Armies of the Hellenistic States 323 BC to AD 30

Armies of the Hellenistic States 323 BC to AD 30

History, Organization & Equipment

Gabriele Esposito

Pen & Sword
MILITARY

First published in Great Britain in 2019 by
Pen & Sword Military
An imprint of
Pen & Sword Books Ltd
Yorkshire – Philadelphia

Copyright © Gabriele Esposito 2019

ISBN 978 1 52673 029 9

The right of Gabriele Esposito to be identified as
Author of this Work has been asserted by him in accordance
with the Copyright, Designs and Patents Act 1988.

A CIP catalogue record for this book is
available from the British Library

Typeset in Ehrhardt
by Mac Style

Printed and bound in India by Replika Press Pvt. Ltd.

Pen & Sword Books Limited incorporates the imprints of Atlas, Archaeology,
Aviation, Discovery, Family History, Fiction, History, Maritime, Military, Military
Classics, Politics, Select, Transport,
True Crime, Air World, Frontline Publishing, Leo Cooper, Remember When,
Seaforth Publishing, The Praetorian Press, Wharncliffe
Local History, Wharncliffe Transport, Wharncliffe True Crime
and White Owl.

For a complete list of Pen & Sword titles please contact

PEN & SWORD BOOKS LIMITED
47 Church Street, Barnsley, South Yorkshire, S70 2AS, England
E-mail: enquiries@pen-and-sword.co.uk
Website: www.pen-and-sword.co.uk

Or

PEN AND SWORD BOOKS
1950 Lawrence Rd, Havertown, PA 19083, USA
E-mail: Uspen-and-sword@casematepublishers.com
Website: www.penandswordbooks.com

Contents

Gabriele Esposito is a military historian who works as a freelance author and researcher for some of the most important publishing houses in the military history sector. In particular, he is an expert specializing in uniformology: his interests and expertise range from the ancient civilizations to modern post-colonial conflicts. During recent years he has conducted and published several researches on the military history of the Latin American countries, with special attention to the War of the Triple Alliance and the War of the Pacific. He is among the leading experts on the military history of the Italian Wars of Unification and the Spanish Carlist Wars. His books and essays are published on a regular basis by Osprey Publishing, Winged Hussar Publishing and Libreria Editrice Goriziana; he is also the author of numerous military history articles appearing in specialized magazines like *Ancient Warfare Magazine*, *Medieval Warfare Magazine*, *The Armourer*, *History of War*, *Guerres et Histoire*, *Focus Storia* and *Focus Storia Wars*.

Acknowledgements

This book is dedicated to my beloved parents, Maria Rosaria and Benedetto, for their immense love and great support in every phase of my life. Thanks to their precious advice, the present book is a much better product: their great intelligence is always a secure guide for me.

A very special mention goes to the German re-enactment group and living history association 'Hetairoi', for providing me with the magnificent and detailed photos that illustrate this book. Without their incredible work of research and re-enactment, the present work would have not been the same. In particular, I want to express my deep gratitude to Thorsten Schillo: he enjoyed and supported the idea of this book from the beginning and helped me in every phase of the production with great generosity and patience.

Introduction

The main aim of this book is to present a detailed overview of the history and organization of the Hellenistic Armies, from the death of Alexander the Great to the fall of Ptolemaic Egypt. In order to understand the nature of Hellenistic military forces, however, the author has decided to start his analysis from the military reforms of Philip of Macedon and Alexander the Great: without describing these, in fact, it is practically impossible to make a proper study on the evolution of the Hellenistic military models. As a result, the first two chapters of this book will be devoted to events that happened before our chronological limit of 323 BC. Similarly, the analysis of this book will go beyond 30 BC for some of the minor Hellenistic armies. The fall of Ptolemaic Egypt is considered by most modern scholars as the symbolic end of the Hellenistic world, since the Ptolemies were the last of the great Hellenistic dynasties to be defeated by Rome (after the Antigonids of Macedonia and the Seleucids of Syria). In any case, as readers of this book will discover, some minor Hellenistic states survived well after 30 BC (mostly as client states of Rome). We will follow the military history of these smaller countries until their final eclipse, thus extending the general period taken into account to the first century AD.

From a geographical point of view, all the Hellenistic armies are included in the present analysis: the lesser-known states, which were located at the borders of the Hellenistic world, are also covered in detail. When Alexander the Great conquered the Persian Empire, the Macedonians acquired an immense territory that included all the Middle East and large parts of Asia; in addition, they also conquered Egypt and retained control over most of the southern Balkans. As a result, the Macedonian Empire was the greatest one that human history had ever seen. Each of the new states that were created after the death of Alexander the Great has been analysed in a specific chapter, generally dealing both with its general history and its military history. For each of the armies taken into account the author has provided an organizational guide as well as several orders of battle. The equipments and weapons used by the various Hellenistic troop types are covered in the various chapters; for more details about this specific aspect, the author suggests that readers pay particular attention to the photographs illustrating the text.

   The book comprises fifteen chapters: the first two, as mentioned above, are dedicated to the description of the Macedonian Army under Philip and Alexander. The third chapter is devoted to the military campaigns fought after the death of Alexander the Great, with special attention to the role of each 'Successor'; the fourth one describes the main wars that were fought during the early decades of the Hellenistic period (before the ascendancy of Rome). The fifth chapter deals with the armies of the early 'Successors' that fought in the wars described in chapters three and four. Starting from chapter six, the book describes the military organization of the three main Hellenistic states: Antigonid Macedonia (chapter six), Ptolemaic Egypt (chapter seven) and the Seleucid Empire (chapter eight). The analysis then moves to Anatolia/Asia Minor, one of the centres of Hellenism: chapter nine deals with the Kingdom of Pergamon (which was formed at the end of the wars between the Successors); chapter ten describes the military history and organization of the smaller Anatolian states (Bithynia, Cappadocia and Galatia); chapter eleven is an analysis of the lesser-known but quite important Hellenistic countries located around the Black Sea and the Caucasus (Kingdom of Pontus, Kingdom of Armenia and the Bosporan Kingdom). Chapter twelve brings the reader back to Europe, to analyse the military forces of Epirus (the 'poor brother' of Macedonia) and the campaigns of Pyrrhus (the real 'heir' of Alexander the Great's legend). Chapter thirteen covers the military organization of the Greek cities located in mainland Greece and southern Italy, which remained significant military powers during the Hellenistic period. Chapter fourteen analyses the role of Israel in the Hellenistic military world, from the great Jewish rebellion against the Seleucids. The final chapter deals with the most peripheral countries of the Hellenistic world: the Bactrian Kingdom (which seceded from the Seleucids like Israel) and the Indo-Greek Kingdom. The author hopes that the readers will like this long 'cavalcade' in the Hellenistic world.

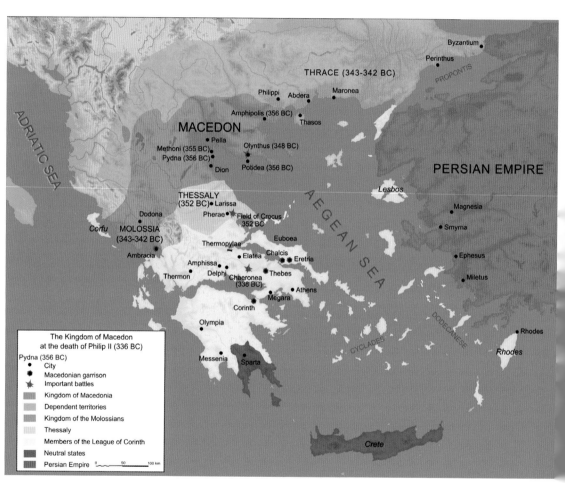

The Kingdom of Macedonia at the death of Philip II. (*CC BY-SA 3.0, Wikimedia User 'MinisterForBadTimes'*)

Chapter 1

The Military Revolution of Philip of Macedon

When Philip II of the Argead dynasty became King of Macedonia in 359 BC, at the age of 23, his country was by no means an important actor of the Greek political scene. Macedonia was located on the northern borders of the Greek world and thus was considered as a semi-civilised kingdom by most of the Greek city-states. In effect, the Macedonian state had originated as a tribal kingdom that was not very different from the smaller ones that were located around it. Over the centuries the Macedonians had progressively adopted Greek culture, but their tribal origins were still clearly visible in their political and social structures. One of the key features of the Macedonians was their innate propensity to war, the result of centuries of open conflict against neighbouring tribes living in the central Balkans. In particular, the Kingdom of Macedonia was surrounded by the following warlike peoples: the Illyrians in the west, the Paeonians and Agrianes in the north (both peoples of mixed Illyrian-Thracian descent) and the Thracians in the east. More or less every year the Macedonian state was under attack from one of these local enemies, who were able to conduct guerrilla operations with great success and for long periods. In addition, the Kingdom of Macedonia was continuously influenced in its internal politics by interference from the most powerful Greek city-states (in particular Sparta, which was the main ally of the Macedonians for several decades before the ascendancy of Philip). From this general description it is very easy to understand why the Kingdom of Macedonia needed to be totally reformed from a military point of view in order to survive: it was important to take a definitive decision for the future, to determine if Macedonia was to become a Greek political power or a state with interests in the interior areas of the Balkans. Philip, who was held as a hostage in Thebes during three years of his youth (368–365 BC), had no doubts about the choice to make once he became king. We will soon see how his decision had very important effects on the military structures of Macedonia. Since the beginning of his reign, Philip's greatest ambition was that of conquering and unifying Greece under Macedonian rule; to achieve this objective, he needed to reform the military apparatus of his state and secure the position of Macedonia in the Balkans (by defeating once and for all the incursions of the neighbouring tribes).

Philip II of Macedon, reconstructed according to the archaeological finds of the Vergina tomb (where the king was buried). (*Photo and copyright by Hetairoi*)

Before the ascendancy of Philip, the Macedonian Army was mostly known in Greece for the great quality of its cavalry; the infantry was little more than a poorly equipped and badly trained band of peasants (not comparable to the elite heavy infantry hoplites of the Greek cities). Differently from most of the Greek states, Macedonia could count on a good number of horses and plains on which to train and deploy them, a factor that made its cavalry superior to any similar force deployed in Greece (with the sole exception of Thessaly). Apparently, during the early decades of the fourth century BC, the Macedonian kings had already started to attempt a reform of their infantry forces: in view of a future confrontation with the armies of the Greek world, the light infantry used to fight the northern tribes of the Balkans would have proved to be of no military use. As a result, presumably during the reign of King Archelaus (413-399 BC), the Macedonians started to organize and train their infantrymen as hoplites in perfect Greek style. When Philip ascended to the throne in 359, the Macedonian Army included more or less 600 cavalrymen and 10,000 infantrymen; only a small portion of the latter were equipped as hoplites, with the majority of the foot troops still composed of shepherds and farmers armed like light infantry skirmishers (in Illyrian or Thracian style). Philip decided to change this situation and transform his army into a combined force of shock troops, with heavy cavalry and heavy infantry playing a prominent role. As a result, he created two main bodies of 'regular' troops: the *pezhetairoi*, or 'foot companions', and the *hetairoi* ('horse companions'). These were to become the nucleus of Alexander the Great's army and the key to its successes.

The military reform of Philip was a very difficult process that only a man with the great personal and military capabilities that he possessed could complete: the starting point, in fact, was very far from the expectations of the new king. According to Macedonian laws, each able-bodied male subject of the king was available for military service as an infantryman, but the quality of these foot soldiers was generally quite poor. The majority of them were equipped as light infantry peltasts, i.e. skirmishers armed with javelins and small shields of the 'pelte' type (a crescent-shaped wicker shield). In practice, the Macedonian infantrymen were virtually indistinguishable from their Illyrian or Thracian enemies and totally unprepared for a campaign of conquest against the Greek cities. Philip soon understood that the only way to defeat his tribal enemies was to create a superior military force, with new tactics and equipment that would surprise them on the field of battle. During the three years that he spent in Thebes as a hostage, Philip had perfectly learned Greek tactical principles and the military innovations introduced by Epaminondas and Iphicrates. The latter had gradually transformed the traditional Greek hoplite from a heavy infantryman into a medium infantryman, by changing some components of their personal equipment. In general terms, the so-called 'Iphicratean hoplite' was a mix between the traditional hoplite

Philip II of Macedon; both the
Macedonian-Phrygian helmet and
the torso armour are made of iron.
The latter is richly ornamented
with gilded embellishments.
(*Photo and copyright by Hetairoi*)

and the light infantry peltast: the length of spears and swords was increased, while the heavy round shield ('hoplon') was substituted by a new smaller and lighter one. Since the new smaller shields could be strapped to the right forearm, the left hand of each soldier was left free to help with holding the new longer spears. The general reduction in the dimensions of the shield gave a higher degree of mobility to these new hoplites, which was further increased by the generalized adoption of linen cuirasses in place of the previous bronze ones. The new kind of shield, despite having different shape and dimensions, was still called 'pelte', like that carried by peltasts. The main result of the Iphicratean reform (taking place in the second half of the fourth century BC) was the adoption of more aggressive tactical approaches by these new infantrymen.

When starting the reform of his infantry, Philip decided to transform his foot soldiers into 'Iphicratean hoplites': he did this thanks to the decisive help of some Greek mercenary officers, who imported the drill and discipline of the Greek citizen armies into the Kingdom of Macedonia. The new infantrymen were the key factor in Philip's subsequent victories over the enemy tribes of the Balkans: for the first time in their history, the Macedonian soldiers had been able to achieve a global superiority over their warlike neighbours. As we have already said, the creation of the 'foot companions' and 'horse companions' was vital for the military reforms of Philip: thanks to their formation, the Macedonian kings could now count on a solid core of regular and professional troops. The *pezhetairoi* totalled 9,000 and were organized into six regiments (*taxeis*) of 1,500 men each; the single *taxeis* comprised three battalions (*lochoi*) with 500 soldiers each. The *lochoi* were usually divided into two blocks of 256 men, known as *syntagmata*: each *syntagma* corresponded to a phalanx, with its 256 soldiers being deployed into sixteen files of sixteen men each. The single *syntagma* was divided into sixteen basic units known as *dekas* and corresponding to the single files. Each regiment of the 'foot companions' was raised from a different district of Macedonia, from which it took its official denomination; the battalions (*lochoi*), instead, were named after their commanders. In total, considering that each regiment of the *pezhetairoi* could deploy six phalanxes, the whole division of the 'foot companions' could field a total of fifty-four phalanxes with 256 soldiers each. Thanks to the introduction of standard equipment and constant training, Philip of Macedon was able to create a new class of professional foot soldiers in a very short time. The 'foot companions' were raised among the peasantry of the kingdom and thus were composed of men having good temperament and excellent physical conditions. After completing the transformation of his original 10,000 infantrymen into the new regular force of the 'foot companions', Philip was ready to fight against the Greek cities and their armies of hoplites. As military events would soon show, the Macedonian phalangist proved to be better-trained and equipped than any opposing Greek fighter.

Pezhetairoi with 'pelte' shields and long 'sarissae' spears. (*Photo and copyright by Hetairoi*)

As regards cavalry, Philip's starting point was much better than for the infantry. As we have already seen, the Macedonian cavalry fielded more or less 600 horsemen: these were mainly upper-class inhabitants of the kingdom, who were economically able to acquire and maintain armour and horses. It is interesting to note, however, that a certain part of them were non-nobles of any origin who enjoyed the trust and friendship of the Macedonian kings and thus had the privilege to serve at the monarch's side. Philip gave to these soldiers, who were already an elite, a proper military structure and increased their numbers. The new regular cavalry of the 'horse companions' was organized in eight squadrons known as *ilai*; each of these comprised 200 horsemen, with the exception of the elite squadron called *basilike ile* (Royal Squadron) or *agema* (Vanguard). The latter had 400 men and acted as the personal mounted guard of the Macedonian kings. The eight cavalry squadrons of the 'horse companions' were considered as an independent cavalry regiment. Apparently each squadron was divided into two sections of 100 men each, excepting for the *agema* that had four sections. Each section was in turn divided into two *tetrarchiai* of fifty soldiers. Like the infantry regiments of the 'foot companions', the *ilai* were recruited on a territorial basis according to the districts of Macedonia. The Royal Squadron, differently from the others, was formed solely by aristocrats from the most important noble families of Macedonia; these personal friends of the king (*philoi*) were named for life by the same monarch. As a result, the *agema* contained the best horsemen from all the districts of the kingdom and was commanded by the same king. The various *ilai* of the 'horse companions' were named after their commanders and could be sometimes grouped together into a larger cavalry formation of three or four squadrons, which was known as *hipparchy*. As is clear from this description, Philip had been able to increase the number of Macedonian cavalrymen from 600 to 1,800 in a relatively short period: his new cavalry, perfectly equipped and trained, was to act as 'shock troops' during large pitched battles and proved to be a decisive element in the military victories of his son, Alexander. In total, we could say that the new Macedonian Army of Philip included seven 'regular' regiments: one of 'horse companions' and six of 'foot companions'.

After the first phase of his military reforms, Philip of Macedon decided to create another new regiment of infantry, known as the 'Regiment of the Royal Hypaspists'. The Hypaspists were elite light infantrymen equipped with the traditional hoplite shield but without armour; apparently Philip decided to form this new unit in order to use it as a flexible link between the 'foot companions' and the 'horse companions'. When the cavalry advanced, the Hypaspists could move forward rapidly in order to keep up with the horsemen: the heavy infantrymen of the phalanxes were too slow in their close formations and thus could not move with the same pace of the cavalry. The Hypaspists were Philip's solution to this serious problem of mobility of the phalangists, since their main function was avoiding the formation of dangerous gaps between the *pezhetairoi* and the *hetairoi*. The Greek word *hypaspist* means 'shield-bearer' and was used to identify this new category of soldiers because they carried large hoplite shields, unlike the 'foot companions' who were equipped with the smaller 'pelte' shield. Originally it seems that the 'Regiment of the Royal Hypaspists' was formed from the personal retainers of the king already included in the 'foot companions': this hypothesis is confirmed by the fact that, at least at the beginning, the new unit was also known as 'The Hypaspists of the Companions'. The regiment had a larger establishment than the normal *taxeis*, being composed of 3,000 elite soldiers, organized into six battalions (*lochoi*) with 500 soldiers each. The Hypaspists of the vanguard battalion had a higher status than those from the other *lochoi* and were known as 'The Royal Hypaspists': these 500 men were selected out of the whole Macedonian Army for their height. This chosen *lochos* guarded the king's tent on the field and always took the place of honour in the battle-line. In all aspects, it was the foot equivalent of the mounted Royal Squadron. The absence of armour made the Hypaspists a category of extremely mobile troops, being balanced by the presence of the large 'hoplon' shield (the only personal protection carried by these men). Apparently, they also acted as a sort of military police inside the army.

Chapter 2

The Macedonian Army of Alexander the Great

Alexander the Great ascended to the throne of Macedon in 336 BC, at the age of 20. The army that he inherited from his father was a perfect military machine, but the military genius of the new monarch was able to improve its quality and performances in many aspects. Before analysing the innovations introduced by Alexander, however, we should describe the other minor or 'non-regular' components of the Macedonian Army already existing under Philip. The first of these was the Royal Bodyguard, or *somatophylax*, which was formed by just seven men drawn from the most important families of the Macedonian aristocracy. These few bodyguards acted both as personal protectors of the king and as high-ranking military officers, holding important command positions such as general. This unit was more or less a sort of staff corps that collaborated with the king. Members of the Royal Bodyguard had to serve in another unit known as the 'Royal Pages' before entering the ranks of the elite *somatophylax*. Since the times of Philip, the sons of the Macedonian nobility who had reached adolescence had to be enrolled in the 'Royal Pages'; these young men had to live at court, where they served as a strong guarantee of their parents' loyalty towards the royal family. In many aspects the corps of the 'Royal Pages' was a sort of military academy, since its members were given a general education in philosophy and other liberal disciplines but also practised hunting and para-military training (including sports). The period of service in the 'Royal Pages' was used to inculcate obedience and deference to the king into the noble youth of Macedonia; as a result, the pages were called upon to perform duties that were not so different from those of the court's slaves. On leaving the 'Royal Pages', the young men would either become members of the Royal Bodyguard or enter the ranks of the 'horse companions' regiment.

Regarding cavalry, it is important to note that the 'horse companions' were only one of the six components that made up the Macedonian mounted troops; the others were: Thessalian cavalry, Greek cavalry, Thracian cavalry, *Prodromoi* (light cavalry) and mercenary cavalry. Thessaly was the only region of Greece having large plains that were perfect for breeding horses, and thus was the only area of the southern Balkans where the local rulers could field large cavalry armies. Thessaly was located just south of Macedonia and had always had very strong link with Alexander the Great's kingdom well before the times of his father, Philip. Different from the Macedonians, the Thessalians

Pezhetairoi bearing the 'Argead Star' (symbol of the Macedonian royal house) on their small round shields. (*Photo and copyright by Hetairoi*)

fielded large contingents of excellent light cavalry armed with javelins: as a result, the tactical combination of heavy 'horse companions' and light Thessalian cavalrymen soon became one of Alexander's keys to success. Before the ascendancy of Macedonia, Thessaly was still only partly urbanized and was dominated by an aristocracy of local nobles who based their personal power on numerous cavalry forces. Traditionally the region of Thessaly had always been divided into four semi-independent provinces, which recognized a sort of formal supreme authority of an elected ruler known as *tagos*. We could describe Thessaly as a sort of confederation: when the ruling *tagos* was strong, the provinces were under central control; when the *tagos* had limited political capabilities, each province acted as an independent state. Civil wars were very frequent and complete anarchy was always just around the corner. Philip of Macedon, called in to support the Thessalians during a conflict against other Greeks, intelligently obtained complete support from the local aristocracy and was later elected as *tagos*. As a result of these political moves, Thessaly soon became an extremely loyal vassal state of Macedonia and provided Alexander with the best allied military contingents sent by the Greeks. When Alexander invaded Asia to attack the Persian Empire, the Macedonian Army comprised a total of 1,800 Thessalian light cavalrymen, these elite soldiers being organized very similarly to the 'horse companions', being structured in a regiment with eight *ilai* (squadrons). As with the Macedonian *hetairoi*, the elite first squadron had 400 soldiers, while all the others comprised 200 men. The vanguard squadron, the Thessalian equivalent of the *agema*, was that formed by Pharsalians (who were considered a real elite, the best horsemen of Greece).

After defeating Athens and Thebes at the Battle of Chaeronea (338 BC), Philip of Macedon asserted his political control over Greece by creating a military alliance known as the League of Corinth. According to the peace treaty signed in 338 by the defeated Greek cities, all members of this new military alliance/federation had to send military contingents when required by the Macedonian kings. In view of the imminent expedition against Persia, Alexander obviously fully employed the military resources of his Greek allies. Regarding cavalry, we should point out that the contribution given by the League of Corinth was quite scarce: just 600 horsemen organized into three squadrons (*ilai*) of 200 soldiers each. It is important to bear in mind, however, that unlike in Macedon or Thessaly, cavalry warfare was not an important component of the Greek military tradition. The first squadron of Greek cavalry comprised Peloponnesian and Achaean cavalrymen; the second was made up by men coming from Phthiotis and Malis (in central Greece); the third was formed with Locrian and Phocian horsemen. Since no city of Greece was able to form and maintain a squadron of cavalry alone, these three units were formed by assembling together the various contingents sent from a particular area of Greece. During most of Alexander's campaign against the

Phalangist with Macedonian-Attic helmet and leather muscle cuirass. (*Photo and copyright by Hetairoi*)

Persian Empire, the three squadrons of Greek cavalry were always employed together and formed an independent *hipparchy* (cavalry brigade). During the later phases of the campaign against the Persians, a second brigade of Greek cavalry was raised in Greece and sent to Asia in order to support the Macedonian Army. Like the existing one, this comprised three squadrons of 200 men each: the first was formed with Boeotians, the second with Acarnanians and Aetolians, the third with Eleians. Apparently, both brigades of allied Greek cavalry included heavy horsemen equipped more or less like the Macedonian 'horse companions'.

The Thracians, who had became allies of Macedonia after Philip's striking victories over them, contributed to Alexander's expedition in Asia by providing three squadrons of light cavalry. The Thracians were famous for their light troops, both mounted and on foot: these were considered as the best skirmishers of the ancient world, and the Greeks had learned most of their light infantry tactics from them. The Greek peltasts, for example, were a simple copy of the standard Thracian light infantry skirmishers. At the time of Philip and Alexander, Thrace was divided into a series of small tribal kingdoms that were constantly at war with each other; two of these, vassals of Macedonia, contributed by sending cavalry soldiers. The Paeonian tribe sent a single squadron under the command of a prince from the Paeonian royal family, while the Odrysian tribe sent two squadrons that were put under the orders of a Macedonian officer. All the Thracian cavalrymen were armed as skirmishers, with javelins and light equipment.

If the heavy cavalry of the Macedonian Army (the 'horse companions') was provided by the aristocracy of the kingdom, the light cavalry of the *Prodromoi* came from the inhabitants of the new Thracian provinces annexed by Philip. Until the reign of the latter, in fact, it seems that the light component of the Macedonian Army's cavalry was very weak. With the annexation of significant Thracian territories, however, Philip was able to recruit a good number of local mounted skirmishers and include them in his own army to form a body of light cavalry. Literally, the word *Prodromoi* means 'scouts', giving a very good idea of the important tactical role played by these soldiers. In total the *Prodromoi* comprised 800 men, organized into four squadrons of 200 men each; their officers were all of Macedonian descent and they were completely separate from the three allied squadrons of Thracian cavalry. Being mostly Thracians, the *Prodromoi* had the same great skirmishing capabilities as the Paeonians and Odrysians; unlike the latter, however, they were much more disciplined and better-trained.

By the times of Philip and Alexander the use of mercenaries was very common in Greece, since the traditional way of warfare based on the primary role played by the citizens/hoplites was in a state of progressive decay. Many Greek cities preferred using mercenaries instead of raising their own contingents of hoplites; in addition,

Phalangist with Phrygian helmet
and leather muscle cuirass.
(*Photo and copyright by Hetairoi*)

several regions of Greece (the poorest ones) had progressively become specialized in providing mercenary contingents to the Persian Empire. The Persians, who had a terrible period of civil wars after their failed campaigns against Greece, soon learned to admire the military capabilities of the Greek hoplites and their superior tactics. As a result, thousands of Greek mercenaries were recruited by the Persian authorities and included in the Imperial Army of the Achaemenids (like the famous 'Ten Thousand' commanded by Xenophon). During the campaign of Alexander against Darius III of Persia, for example, the Macedonians had to face a large contingent of Greek mercenary infantry serving under their enemies. It seems that the Greek mercenary cavalry employed by Alexander the Great was entirely composed of light horsemen. The Macedonian Army that invaded Asia initially included just a single squadron of mercenary cavalry, which was later left as a garrison in Anatolia and thus played no part in the following military operations. With the progression of hostilities, however, Alexander felt a strong need for more light cavalry troops: as a result, two brigades of mercenary Greek cavalry, with two squadrons each, were formed before the decisive Battle of Gaugamela. Later in the war, when the Macedonian Army reached the city of Ecbatana, the squadrons of allied Greek cavalry were disbanded; their members, however, were encouraged to continue service under Alexander and thus to enter the ranks of the Greek mercenary cavalry. With the inclusion of many of these men the mercenary cavalry was expanded, with the creation of a third brigade, always made up of two squadrons. At the beginning of his campaigns in Asia, Alexander considered the mercenary cavalrymen as expendable soldiers of low quality, but over time he started to appreciate the great military capabilities shown by these professionals on several occasions. Generally speaking, the mercenary horsemen gradually reached the same standards of service of the other light cavalry contingents.

Regarding the infantry, we should bear in mind that it was not composed only of the 'foot companions' and Hypaspists described above. The Macedonian Army also included two other categories of foot soldiers: the Greek allies/mercenaries and the light infantrymen. When Alexander attacked the Persian Empire, the Macedonian Army invading Asia included a total of 7,000 Greek heavy infantrymen sent by the League of Corinth. This large allied corps was formed by several different contingents sent by each of the Greek cities that were part of the League; each Greek city-state contributed according to the human resources that were available. These contingents were formed by chosen soldiers known as *epilektoi*, who were selected from among the best men at the service of each city. Each Greek contingent served under its own officers, but the whole body of 7,000 Greek infantrymen was under control of a Macedonian supreme commander. In addition, like for the cavalry, the Macedonian Army included a large number of mercenary Greek infantrymen: these were mostly

Phalangist with Pilos helmet and linen cuirass ('linothorax'). Note the peculiar practice of dividing the 'sarissa' in two parts. (*Photo and copyright by Hetairoi*)

employed as garrison troops, being stationed in the newly conquered provinces of Asia while the Macedonian Army advanced further east. Once in Asia, Alexander recruited several hundred Greek mercenaries who had previously been part of the Persian Army. Unlike with the hired cavalry, infantry mercenaries frequently proved to be unreliable soldiers and often revolted against the Macedonians. At the Battle of Gaugamela, Alexander deployed two infantry regiments of mercenaries: the first of these included 5,000 men, while the other had 4,000 (bringing the total of Greek foot soldiers inside the Macedonian Army to 16,000, allies or mercenaries). The first regiment was considered an elite unit, its members being known as *archaioi* (veterans), due to the fact that these 5,000 soldiers were the original nucleus of mercenaries that departed from Greece at the beginning of the Asian campaigns. The other regiment was known as the 'Achaean' one, since its 4,000 components were all recruited in the northern Peloponnese (one of the poorest regions of Greece, famous for exporting mercenaries). This second regiment joined Alexander's forces only at a later stage. The majority of the Greek infantrymen, be they allies or mercenaries, were equipped as traditional hoplites (albeit having lighter personal equipment than previously).

The light infantrymen of the Macedonian Army were called *psiloi* and were equipped as skirmishers, armed with javelins or slings. Apparently they were organized into large companies of 500 men each, but it seems that the number of companies varied widely. Contrary to the heavy infantry of the 'foot companions' and the Hypaspists, the *psiloi* fought in open order and mostly acted as scouts or skirmishers. In addition to these, the Macedonian Army included separate units of archers (*toxotai*), with three companies of 500 men each. All the companies were assembled into the 'Corps of Archers', which was under overall command of a single officer. The first company was formed by Cretans, while the other two were made up of Macedonians. The Cretan archers were probably mercenaries, since the island of Crete was famous in the ancient world as the homeland of the best Greek archers. Cretan mercenaries were employed on the continent by several of the most important Greek city-states, earning a very good military reputation thanks to their skills and professionalism. These professional soldiers continued to be employed on a large scale by the Hellenistic States emerging after the collapse of Alexander's empire and were an important component of the Roman Army during the period of the Late Republic/Early Empire. Finally, the light infantry of the Macedonian Army also contained several allied contingents sent by the Illyrian and Thracian tribes: these excellent skirmishers were not equipped as the *psiloi* but were traditional peltasts. Apparently the Agrianes were the best of these contingents at the disposal of Alexander, being used to light infantry warfare in mountainous terrain. It seems that the crack peltasts of the Agrianes came from the household troops of the local king (a vassal of Macedonia), and thus were chosen

Phalangist with 'pelte' shield.
(*Photo and copyright by Hetairoi*)

soldiers. The Agrianes were initially organized into a single company of 500 men, but a second one having the same establishment was later sent to join the Macedonian Army before the Battle of Issus. In addition to the Agrianes, the military forces of Alexander crossing the Hellespont included a total of 7,000 allied light infantrymen. These came from several tribes of allied Illyrians and Thracians, Odrysians and Triballians being among the most important ones. Apparently all these contingents sent by client kings were organized into companies of 500 men like the rest of the light infantry; these units could be commanded by tribal military leaders or by Macedonian officers. Like with the archers, an overall military commander controlled all the allied light infantrymen.

After the decisive Battle of Gaugamela, Alexander the Great started to partially reform the organization of the Macedonian Army in order to face the new military needs of his vast empire. After receiving significant reinforcements from Macedonia and Greece, one of the first new measures was increasing the number of heavy infantry regiments (*taxeis*) to seven by creating a new one. After reaching the city of Ecbatana, as previously said, all the Greek allied forces (including Thessalian cavalry) were disbanded and permitted to go home. Many of the Greeks, especially cavalrymen, decided to remain in Asia and continued to serve under Alexander as mercenaries. Some time later, once the conquest of the Persian Empire had been completed, Alexander started to recruit soldiers from his new subjects of Asia: shortly before his death, he was able to assemble and train a large body of 30,000 young Persian recruits who were known as *Epigoni*. These infantrymen were trained and equipped as Macedonian phalangists, but it seems that they took part in no major military actions before the death of Alexander and their subsequent disappearance. After Gaugamela, the Macedonian Army started to also include some units of local light cavalrymen recruited from the populations living in the eastern provinces of the former Persian Empire. These soldiers, generally armed with javelins, were called *hippakontistai*. During Alexander's last military campaign in India, the elite 'Regiment of the Royal Hypaspists' received silver-plated shields in reward for its excellent military service during several years of campaigning in Asia; as a result, the unit changed its name to *Argyraspides* (literally 'silver shields'). Since 331 BC, the Hypaspists Regiment had been reorganized as three battalions of 1,000 men each, which were known as *chiliarchies*. As we will see in the next chapters, these elite 3,000 veterans continued to have a very important military role after the death of Alexander.

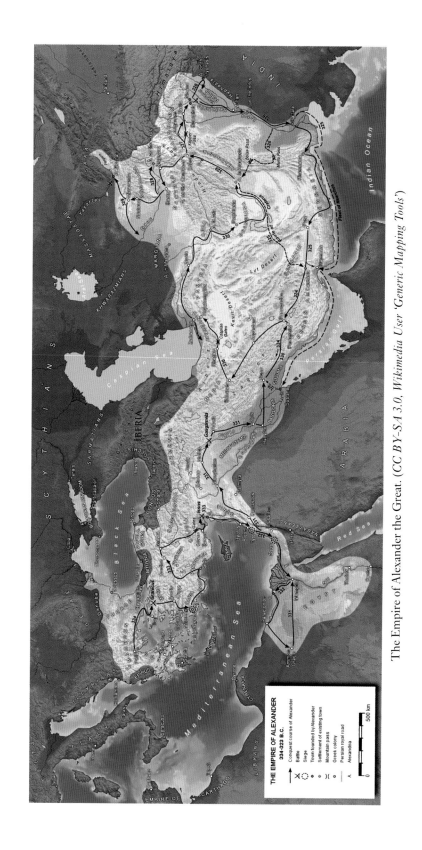

The Empire of Alexander the Great. (*CC BY-SA 3.0, Wikimedia User 'Generic Mapping Tools'*)

Chapter 3

The Succession to Alexander
and the Wars of the Diadochi

Alexander the Great died in the afternoon of 11 June 323 BC, in his magnificent royal palace of Babylon. The conqueror of the Persian Empire had no direct legitimate heirs (his wife Roxane was pregnant but the child was not yet born) and thus a very complicated succession crisis soon began. On the day following Alexander's death, all the most important Macedonian military officers held a public meeting with the objective of finding an heir who could rule the immense fortunes of Asia. The Macedonians were foreigners in a far country and were surrounded by recently conquered populations: a strong political and military leadership was absolutely necessary to ensure the survival of the empire. The most obvious candidate to the throne of Alexander was his half-brother, Philip Arrhidaeus, but he was mentally deficient and epileptic; as a result of this, it was very difficult to find a solution. Perdiccas, the commander of the 'horse companions' who had received from the hands of Alexander the symbolic 'royal ring' before his death, proposed to wait until Roxane had given birth to the legitimate heir. His position, however, was soon opposed by the other officers because he clearly hoped to obtain the regency until the boy grew up. Nearchus, the commander of the Macedonian fleet, pointed out that Alexander already had an heir, albeit not a legitimate one: Heracles, three years of age, son of a concubine named Barsine. This suggestion by Nearchus, however, was not made for the prosperity of the empire but out of personal interest: Nearchus had married a daughter of Barsine and thus would have been very influential if Heracles was to become the new king. Ptolemy, personal friend of the dead king and second-in-command during Alexander's last military campaign, refused the idea of having as ruler of the Macedonian Empire a half-breed like the sons of Roxane and Barsine. Instead he proposed that the future king be chosen by the military leaders assembled at the meeting, in line with ancient Macedonian traditions. Meleager, the commander of the 'foot companions', strongly supported having Philip Arrhidaeus as the new king: in his opinion he was the only candidate of real Macedonian descent and the only one who could rule the empire as a single political body. The various officers supporting Ptolemy's 'democratic' option were all hoping to obtain a division of the immense empire into smaller kingdoms (of which they could become supreme rulers). For some

Phalangist with Pilos helmet. (*Photo and copyright by Hetairoi*)

time the situation was very tense and there was a risk of a civil war between the 'horse companions' and the 'foot companions'. Despite Meleager being killed, the threat of a civil war was temporarily avoided. A sort of compromise was eventually reached: the new king would be Philip Arrhidaeus, with the name of Philip III, until Roxane's baby reached an age to be king (with the name of Alexander IV). Both the present 'fool' king and the future young king were put under the regency of Perdiccas, who effectively became the master of the Macedonian Empire; in exchange for this, he nominated all the other Macedonian military leaders as satraps (provincial governors) of the various territories of the empire.

Very soon, however, this political compromise revealed all its limits: when the Athenians and other Greeks heard that Alexander was dead, they rose in open revolt against the Macedonians. During Alexander's campaigns in Asia, all the Macedonian military forces in Europe (and thus in Greece) were under the supreme command of Antipater, who had gradually increased his political influence over the Macedonian court. Due to the enormous distances involved, however, Antipater had gained nothing from the decisions taken in Babylon soon after Alexander's death. In addition, he now had to face the violent revolt of the Greek cities. During the autumn of 323 BC, the Greeks occupied the strategic pass of Thermopylae and repulsed Antipater's attempt to subdue them; the Macedonian general was defeated and obliged to stay inside the fortress of Lamia with all his remaining forces. As a result the war continued, becoming known as the Lamian War. During the spring of the following year, Antipater was relieved by a Macedonian army coming from Anatolia, but the general situation of the conflict continued to be very negative for the Macedonians. During the summer another Macedonian army arrived from Asia, under the command of general Craterus. Eventually, after months of harsh fighting, the combined forces of Antipater and Craterus were able to defeat the Greeks at the Battle of Crannons (5 September 322 BC). From this moment, the Greek cities were no longer treated as allies by the Macedonians but started to be considered as vassals.

Very soon a new conflict broke out in another area of the Macedonian Empire: Cappadocia (in modern Turkey). The Persian province of Cappadocia had never been fully conquered during Alexander's reign, because the king always pushed his army east and soon lost interest in the western provinces of Anatolia. Cappadocia had remained under the rule of the former Persian satrap, Ariarathes, who recognized Alexander the Great as emperor only to retain his personal dominions. After the death of the king, he soon rose up in open revolt against the authority of Perdiccas. The strategic location of Cappadocia, which was very near to the road connecting Macedonia to Asia, meant that the threat represented by Ariarathes had to be faced as soon as possible. Cappadocia bordered with the satrapy of Phrygia, which was ruled

Phalangist with
Sidon helmet and
no armour. (*Photo
and copyright by
Hetairoi*)

by the Macedonian general Antigonus Monophthalmus. The latter was the first to deal with the Cappadocians, but later abandoned the hostilities when the central army of Perdiccas was sent to crush Ariarathes. Considering the intervention of Perdiccas as an invasion of his sphere of influence, Antigonus decided to abandon Anatolia and went to Macedonia (where he was well received by Antipater and Craterus). During the last weeks of 321 BC, the Macedonian leaders in Europe decided to revolt against Perdiccas: the ensuing conflict was known as the First War of the Diadochi, from the Greek name given to Alexander's successors. The conflict was caused by Perdiccas' refusal to marry the daughter of Antipater, which had been arranged for some time; Perdiccas preferred to marry princess Cleopatra (sister of Alexander the Great and widow of Alexander of Molossis, King of Epirus). The eventual son of Perdiccas and Cleopatra would have been a direct heir of Philip of Macedon and thus would have ruled the whole Macedonian Empire as legitimate monarch. Obviously this possible future was not acceptable for Antipater and most of the other Diadochi. A great military alliance was soon formed against Perdiccas, which included Antipater, Craterus, Antigonus Monophthalmus and Ptolemy (who had ruled until then as the powerful satrap of Egypt). In 320 the four rebel leaders formalized their alliance with some strategic marriages and were joined by Lysimachus, the governor of Thrace. Perdiccas, on the other side, was supported by the new satrap of Cappadocia, Eumenes, the former secretary of Alexander the Great.

The first move of Perdiccas was to attack Europe, sending his army under the command of Eumenes. However, Eumenes had no military experience and was going to face the veteran forces of Antipater and Craterus. In late April, near the Hellespont, Eumenes and Craterus fought each other, and against all expectations Eumenes was able to achieve a clear victory over his more experienced opponent. Craterus was killed in the battle and what remained of his forces went back to join the army of Antipater. Meanwhile, Perdiccas marched at the head of another large army against Ptolemy in Egypt: the powerful regent tried to cross the Nile on two occasions, but his forces were repulsed by Ptolemy. After these military failures and suffering heavy losses, the soldiers of Perdiccas' army rose in revolt against their general. Taking the opportunity given by the revolt, the generals who had followed Perdiccas into Egypt (guided by Seleucus) organized the assassination of the regent with the objective of ending the war. After the death of Perdiccas, Seleucus and the other traitors started negotiations with Ptolemy. The regency was offered to the satrap of Egypt, but he refused it. At this point Antipater decided to intervene in the negotiations, to impose some order into the organization of the empire and obtain more power for himself. A new settlement was made, according to which Antipater became the new regent. Ptolemy was to remain the independent ruler of Egypt, while Seleucus became the

Italic mercenary phalangist with
Apulian helmet and Oscan waistbelt.
(*Photo and copyright by Hetairoi*)

provincial governor of Babylon (the richest city of the empire). Lysimachus was to keep Thrace, with Antigonus receiving complete control over the large territories of Anatolia; consequently it was now Antigonus' task to defeat Eumenes and his victorious army. Curiously, after settling all these affairs, Antipater died in 319 BC. The political and military situation was now set to change again.

On his death bed Antipater nominated an old and experienced military commander, Polyperchon, as the new regent. This unexpected choice, however, was not accepted by Antipater's son, Cassander, who soon revolted against the new authority of Polyperchon and formed an alliance with Ptolemy of Egypt. The Egyptian satrap was attempting to expand his personal dominions by conquering the rich lands of Syria, and thus needed a new *casus belli* to resume the hostilities. This was the beginning of the Second War of the Diadochi, which was even more destructive than the previous one. Cassander and Ptolemy were soon joined by Antigonus in their alliance against Polyperchon. The ruler of Anatolia, like Ptolemy, wanted to be even more independent and conquer new territories in Asia. Being in serious difficulty, Polyperchon was in desperate need of an ally and found it in Eumenes. With a large amount of money and a good number of soldiers, Eumenes marched against Ptolemy in Syria and was able to defeat him in battle. Meanwhile, in Europe, Polyperchon promised political freedom to all the Greek cities in exchange for their loyalty during the new war against Cassander: the majority of the Greeks accepted the offer and sided with Polyperchon, but some strategic locations (including the port of Athens) gave their loyalty to Cassander. In the spring of 317 BC, Cassander was able to gain the upper hand during military operations in Greece and was proclaimed regent of Philip Arridaeus, thus obtaining total control over Macedonia. Polyperchon escaped to the Kingdom of Epirus, located west of Macedonia, which was ruled by the royal family of the Molossi (to which the mother of Alexander the Great, Olympia, belonged). Here he went with Roxane and Alexander the Great's legitimate son, later also being joined by queen Olympia. Although having with him several members of the royal family and being supported by the monarch of Epirus, Polyperchon was by now quite weak from a military point of view. Despite this, while Cassander was campaigning with his forces in the Peloponnese, Polyperchon marched back into Macedonia and killed Philip Arridaeus. In the following year, Cassander obtained some minor victories in Greece and was even able to capture and kill Olympia, but the war against Polyperchon continued.

Regarding the military operations conducted in Asia, we should point out that Antigonus commanded a much larger military force than Eumenes, who was obliged to adopt a defensive policy and was besieged in the fortress of Mora (located in the Taurus Mountains) by the superior forces of Antigonus. At one point it seemed that victory was very near for Antigonus, but when Eumenes was ready to surrender, the

Hypaspist with hoplite spear and Argive
round shield. (*Photo and copyright by Hetairoi*)

forces of Antigonus were obliged to abandon the siege in order to move against a fleet sent by Polyperchon to help his ally. In the autumn of 318 BC, Antigonus defeated the enemy fleet and reconquered the region of Lydia. The decision to abandon the siege of Mora, however, soon proved to be a wrong one because it gave Eumenes the time to escape and gather new military forces. The army of Eumenes then marched across the central provinces of Asia but was attacked by the forces of Seleucus, coming from the satrapy of Babylon. Seleucus had decided to join forces with Cassander and Antigonus. Eumenes was also able to escape from this new attack and went to the important city of Susa, where he met with all the satraps of the eastern provinces. After discussing with the provincial governors, Eumenes was able to convince them of the legitimacy of his position and they sided with him and Polyperchon. Thanks to the support of these eastern satraps, Eumenes was able to face the army of Antigonus on almost equal terms, but the following military operations resulted in a stalemate. In January 316 BC, the hostilities between the two leaders resumed, this time leading to a decisive victory for Antigonus (Eumenes was abandoned by one of his eastern allies during the decisive battle). Eumenes was captured and executed, thus leaving Antigonus as the sole master of Asia. At this point Seleucus understood that if the power of Antigonus continued to increase it would mark the end of his own ambitions. Rather than face being killed, Seleucus abandoned Babylon and fled in exile to Egypt under the protection of Ptolemy. The following years also saw the end of the war in Europe, with the partial defeat of Polyperchon.

The ascendancy of Antigonus caused many worries to Ptolemy, who soon understood that Egypt would be the next target in the expansionist policy carried on by the new ruler of Asia. Ptolemy warned Cassander and Lysimachus (the governor of Thrace) in the hope of convincing them to form an alliance against Antigonus; a treaty between the three leaders was finally signed and a written ultimatum was sent to Antigonus. This was the beginning of the so-called Third War of the Diadochi in the spring of 315 BC. The ruler of Asia immediately seized the initiative by attacking Phoenicia and Syria, but the long siege of Tyre prevented him from invading Egypt. In the meantime, Seleucus, who was now the commander of Ptolemy's fleet, assaulted and conquered the island of Cyprus, annexing it to the possessions of Ptolemy. While fighting in Asia, Antigonus allied himself with Polyperchon, who still controlled some areas of Greece (most notably the Peloponnese). The new alliance with the old Polyperchon was a very positive one for Antigonus, leading to the defeat of Cassander. At this point Antigonus tried to invade Macedonia, but his forces were defeated by those of Lysimachus. In Asia, the siege of Tyre finally came to an end and the city surrendered to Antigonus. Ptolemy, however, had gained enough time to gather new forces and thus was able to repulse the subsequent attempted invasion mounted by Antigonus against Egypt. In

Hypaspist with Macedonian–Attic helmet and bronze muscle cuirass. (*Photo and copyright by Hetairoi*)

December 311 BC, a peace treaty was concluded between the two opposing military alliances, according to which the 'status quo' was formally restored and all the *diadochi* retained their former territories: Ptolemy in Egypt, Lysimachus in Thrace, Cassander in Macedonia, Antigonus in Asia and Polyperchon in the Peloponnese. In addition, both parties agreed to recognize the legitimate son of Alexander the Great and Roxane as the heir to the whole Macedonian Empire once he became of age. However, both Roxane and her son were then killed, their assassination being ordered by Cassander, with the objective of eliminating the last members of the legitimate Macedonian royal house.

In Asia, however, the hostilities continued between Antigonus and Seleucus, the latter marching with the troops under his command from Syria to Babylon in order to recover his former position as satrap of Babylon. Due to the lack of garrison forces, Seleucus was able to occupy the important city without major difficulties. Antigonus initially considered Seleucus and his forces just a secondary menace and thus sent only the local forces of some satraps against them. The governors of Media and Aria marched on Babylon against Seleucus, but were defeated in a large pitched battle fought near the Tigris. Seleucus soon incorporated the defeated enemy soldiers into his army and occupied the provinces of the two satraps loyal to Antigonus. In more or less six months, Seleucus was able to conquer a large part of Antigonus' territories, including Elam and the important city of Susa. These military operations are commonly known as the Babylonian War and were a real turning point in the history of Hellenistic Asia. At this point Antigonus understood that Seleucus was a real menace for his large dominions, and thus sent his son, Demetrius, with a large army to besiege Babylon. The military forces of Demetrius were able to conquer the first citadel of Babylon, but not the second; as a result a long siege started, during which Seleucus conducted continuous guerrilla operations against the besiegers. In August 310 BC, Antigonus arrived at Babylon in a bid to definitively end the war. He launched punitive raids in the countryside around Babylon and organized new assaults against the second citadel, but all these costly military operations came to nothing. Babylon continued to resist and the guerrilla war of Seleucus was not eliminated. Finally, to determine once and for all the future of Asia, the armies of Antigonus and Seleucus fought each other in a large pitched battle: in August 309, after some harsh fighting, Antigonus was defeated and retreated to Syria. A truce, ending the Babylonian War, was signed, but there could be only one ruler in Asia and thus Antigonus and Seleucus were to fight again in the near future. Meanwhile, Seleucus conquered all the eastern satrapies (including Bactria) and even launched an invasion of India.

Taking advantage of Antigonus' absence from the west, Ptolemy and Cassander had gradually developed a new expansionist policy; the former, in particular, had

Hypaspist with Macedonian–Attic helmet and
bronze muscle cuirass. (*Photo and copyright by
Hetairoi*)

invaded the island of Cyprus in 309 BC. Antigonus, however, soon responded, sending the bastard son of Alexander the Great, Heracles, to his old ally Polyperchon in the Peloponnese. Antigonus wanted Polyperchon to use Heracles in order to raise a revolt against Cassander in Greece and Macedonia. However, Polyperchon decided to change sides and abandoned Antigonus, allying himself with Cassander and leaving the young Heracles to his destiny (Cassander soon ordered his assassination). In 307 BC, after these preliminary events, the Fourth War of the Diadochi broke out. Antigonus decided to launch a major offensive in Greece against Cassander, who was considered the weakest part of his enemies: he sent his son, Demetrius, to Athens, who was soon able to gain complete support from most of the Greek cities. In a very short time Cassander lost any form of control over Greece and was obliged to retreat all his forces to the north in order to defend Macedonia. At this point, with the Greek cities on his side and with Cassander defeated, Antigonus turned against Ptolemy in the south. His first target, attacked in the spring of 306, was Cyprus. The invasion force under the command of Demetrius could count on a large number of impressive siege machines. Initially the operation was a great success, but the military forces of Ptolemy were finally able to resist in the citadel of Salamis, the most important city of Cyprus. After some time, Ptolemy arrived with his fleet and many reinforcements to relieve the defenders of Salamis. Now heavily outnumbered, Demetrius made a desperate move and attacked the fleet of Ptolemy before it could join forces with the besieged. Incredibly, Demetrius was able to win and destroy most of the enemy fleet. Ptolemy fled to Egypt and a few days later the last defenders of Cyprus surrendered. After this brilliant victory, it seemed that Antigonus and Demetrius were going to create a powerful new royal house that could rule all the territories of the former Macedonian Empire, but as a result of this all the other *diadochi* formed a new military alliance against them.

At this point Antigonus made a serious mistake: instead of marching against Seleucus, who was becoming increasingly powerful in eastern Asia, he organized the invasion of Egypt. Since no previous attempt to invade Egypt by land had achieved success, Antigonus decided to attack the realm of Ptolemy by assaulting it from the sea. A large fleet, under the command of Demetrius, was assembled and sent against Egypt. Weather conditions, however, were terrible and several storms prevented the fleet of Demetrius from landing troops in Egypt. The invasion was cancelled and the original plan ended in complete failure. In 305 BC, Antigonus and Demetrius decided to take the initiative again and moved against the island of Rhodes, which was ruled as an independent mercantile republic (allied to Cassander and Ptolemy). The fleet of Rhodes was extremely large and powerful, so its destruction was a real priority for Antigonus. By thus obtaining complete control over the Aegean Sea, he could have sent his troops against Cassander in Macedonia; in addition, Rhodes was ready to help

Hypaspist with Attic helmet and composite 'linothorax'. (*Photo and copyright by Hetairoi*)

Ptolemy in the difficult process of reconstructing his fleet (something that Antigonus had to avoid at all costs, in order not to undo the benefits of Demetrius' brilliant naval victory of Cyprus). This time Demetrius and his fleet showed all their great capabilities in siege warfare, but Rhodes resisted thanks to the massive military help sent by the allied *diadochi* (Lysimachus, Cassander and Ptolemy). What had started as a minor operation against a secondary enemy soon became the most important campaign of the war. In the end, after several clashes, the siege of Rhodes was abandoned by Demetrius and a peace treaty concluded with the mercantile republic, according to which Rhodes was now to act as an ally of Antigonus but not against Ptolemy (thus adopting more or less a neutral position during the following conflicts). Meanwhile, Cassander had reorganized his forces in Macedonia and had been able to regain control over most of the Greek cities. Only Athens still resisted, but was under siege. In the autumn of 304 BC, Demetrius landed in Greece and saved Athens. After a few months of campaigning, most of the Greek cities were again liberated from the rule of Cassander, including the Peloponnese, where Polyperchon had recently died.

When Demetrius was on the point of invading Macedonia, however, he had to abandon the operations in Europe in order to face the menaces coming from the east. A truce was concluded with Cassander, who continued to rule Macedonia despite having been expelled from Greece. Lysimachus had invaded western Anatolia, advancing from Thrace, but in the summer of 302 he was trapped between the army of Demetrius coming from Greece and that of Antigonus marching from Syria. When everything seemed lost for Lysimachus, Seleucus arrived from the heart of Asia with a large army that included about 500 war elephants. At this point it became clear that the imminent battle between Demetrius/Antigonus and Lysimachus/Seleucus would have determined the destiny of the Hellenistic world. In 301 BC at Ipsus, in Phrygia, the military forces of Antigonus were decisively defeated: the experienced leader was killed during the battle and his son, Demetrius, was able to escape with only a small number of soldiers. Now Lysimachus and Seleucus could divide the territories of Antigonus between themselves, but also had to consider the presence of Ptolemy. Lysimachus obtained western Anatolia, while Seleucus occupied eastern Anatolia and also marched towards Syria. Ptolemy, however, had already occupied most of Syria while military operations were going on in Phrygia. The Fourth War of the Diadochi was now over, although Demetrius had gone to Greece and was still able to control some land and naval forces.

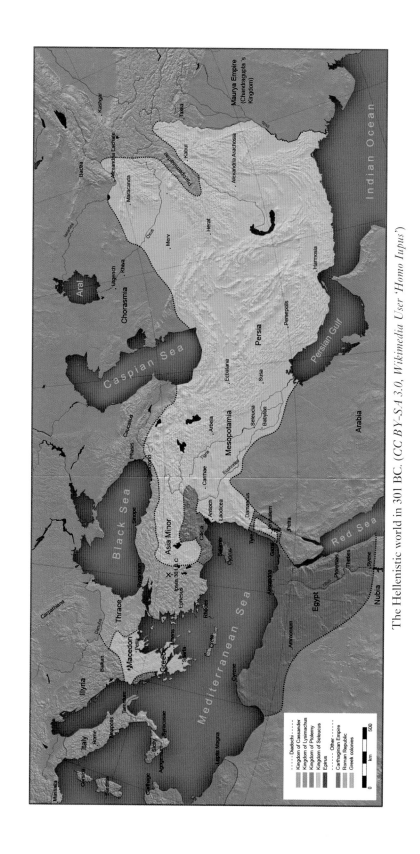

The Hellenistic world in 301 BC. *(CC BY-SA 3.0, Wikimedia User 'Homo lupus')*

Chapter 4

The Wars of the Hellenistic World

In the new political order created after the end of the Fourth War of the Diadochi, the only disturbing element was Demetrius, because despite having been defeated he still controlled the Peloponnese in Greece and the strategic island of Cyprus. In addition, he still commanded a large fleet of excellent warships that could control most of the Mediterranean trade routes. As a result of this situation, all the other Hellenistic monarchs wished to eliminate him as soon as possible. In 300 BC, Ptolemy, Lysimachus and Cassander formed a military alliance against Demetrius, who, in order to avoid complete political isolation, allied himself with Seleucus. It was very clear at the time that Ptolemy and Seleucus were going to fight each other for possession of Syria, and thus Seleucus was in search of an ally. During the following years, Demetrius tried to expand his possessions in Greece. Most of the Greek cities had abandoned him after the defeat of his father and were now allies of Cassander. In 296 BC, Demetrius besieged Athens, taking the city during the following year. Meanwhile, in 298, Cassander had died. The throne of Macedonia had been inherited by his son, Philip, but he died of natural causes just two months into his reign. As a result of this unexpected death, Macedonia was divided into two parts between the younger brothers of Philip: Antipater received western Macedonia and Alexander was given eastern Macedonia. Soon, as expected by Demetrius, the two Macedonian princes started to quarrel, the initial skirmishes transforming into open war. Under strong pressure from his brother, Alexander decided to request the military support of Demetrius and Pyrrhus. The latter had become King of Epirus in 297 BC, thanks to a coup financed by Ptolemy. In 294, Pyrrhus invaded Macedonia and defeated the military forces of Antipater, restoring order. In reward for his intervention, Pyrrhus received the important city of Ambracia in western Greece; in the coming decades, Ambracia became the capital of Epirus. Meanwhile, Demetrius had prepared a military force to intervene in Macedonia and was now marching north from the Peloponnese. Alexander, fearing that Demetrius could now enter Macedonia only to invade it, marched south to meet his uncomfortable ally. Alexander had a plan to kill Demetrius, but this was discovered by the veteran military leader, and as a result it was Alexander who was killed at the meeting. Almost immediately, the Macedonian army joined forces with the troops of Demetrius and proclaimed the latter as King of Macedonia. Demetrius immediately

Thureophoros with Sidon helmet and oval shield. (*Photo and copyright by Hetairoi*)

attacked the western half of Macedonia controlled by Antipater, who was easily defeated and fled to the court of Lysimachus in search of support.

While fighting in Macedonia, Demetrius could do nothing to save Cyprus from the massive invasion launched by Ptolemy, but after having been almost wiped from the political map he was now in full control of Macedonia. During the following years he continued to expand his control over mainland Greece, organizing a series of minor campaigns against various cities. By the end of this process, most of Greece was again under Macedonian dominance (with the notable exceptions of Sparta and Aetolia). When Demetrius tried to attack Aetolia, Pyrrhus moved against him to limit his expansionist policy. The invasion of Aetolia was repulsed, but the war between Demetrius and Pyrrhus continued until 289. In that year, Pyrrhus tried to invade Macedonia and claim the throne of Demetrius for himself, but after being defeated he retreated and signed a peace treaty with his enemy. However, Demetrius had reached the zenith of his power and was soon facing defeat himself. In 288 BC, the population of Macedonia revolted against him, while his former enemies renewed their alliance against him (Ptolemy and Lysimachus were now also joined by Seleucus). In order to retain his kingdom, Demetrius concentrated all his efforts on defeating his external enemies. After destroying the naval forces of Ptolemy, he was able to land with his army in Asia, with the objective of defeating Lysimachus. The initial part of his land campaign was a success, but the situation changed with the arrival of Seleucus in Anatolia. Surrounded by the superior forces of Lysimachus and Seleucus, Demetrius was finally defeated and obliged to surrender; he was captured by Seleucus, his former ally, in 286. The defeat of Demetrius created a new political problem: who was going to rule the Kingdom of Macedonia, Lysimachus from Thrace or Pyrrhus from Epirus?

We should remember that Demetrius had a son, Antigonus Gonatas, who, despite having been obliged to abandon Macedonia, remained in control of Greece. War between Lysimachus and Pyrrhus seemed inevitable in 285 BC, but against all odds the two kings found a compromise and avoided open war: Pyrrhus gained some territories but abandoned his claims over Macedonia, realising the military forces of Lysimachus were clearly superior to his troops. In 282 Ptolemy died, leaving the throne of Egypt to his younger son, Ptolemy Philadelphus. Ptolemy Keraunos, the eldest son of Ptolemy, was shocked by the decision of his father and fled to the court of Seleucus. The latter, hoping that one day Ptolemy Keraunos could become his puppet monarch of Egypt, promised to support the claims of Ptolemy's eldest son. Now that Egypt was quite weak and Demetrius had disappeared from the scene, Seleucus understood that he had a chance to recreate the Macedonian Empire of Alexander the Great: his only obstacle was Lysimachus, who now ruled Macedonia and Anatolia in addition to Thrace. During the last months of 282 BC, Seleucus moved against the Asian provinces of Lysimachus

Thureophoros with spear and a couple of javelins. (*Photo and copyright by Hetairoi*)

After a year of campaigning, the two old military leaders and allies of many conflicts fought against each other at Corupedium in February 281. Seleucus was the victor and Lysimachus was killed during the battle. It now seemed that Seleucus was the real heir of Alexander the Great, the only man who could unify the whole Hellenistic world. However, the jealousy of one man prevented such dreams of unification: Ptolemy Keraunos, fearing the increasing power of his protector, assassinated Seleucus. The events of 281 led to a political stabilization inside the Hellenistic world. Seleucus was replaced on the throne of Asia by his son, Antiochus, while the possessions of Lysimachus were taken by Ptolemy Keraunos. Ptolemy Philadelphus remained stable in Egypt, while Antigonus Gonatas continued to rule most of Greece. The only kingdom lacking a precise political identity was that of the usurper Ptolemy Keraunos; the other three seemed more stable. During the period 280-279 BC, Ptolemy Philadelphus and Antiochus fought each other (exactly like their fathers) for possession of Syria, but this First Syrian War came to nothing and the *status quo* remained in the region.

Soon after assuming control of Lysimachus' possessions, Ptolemy Keraunos had to face a serious menace coming from the heart of the Balkans. This time, however, the threat was not an internal one coming from the same Hellenistic world. Thrace was invaded by the Celts, who were migrating from the woods of central Europe and were in search of new lands to raid and conquer. The Celts who invaded Thrace were known as Galatians and were fierce warriors: they fought with weapons and tactics that the Hellenistic troops had never faced before, so they were able to obtain several unexpected victories during the first phase of their invasion. Ptolemy Keraunos was no match for the Galatians, partly because he knew very little of his new dominions. Lysimachus had been able to rule Thrace thanks only to his perfect knowledge of the local tribes, something that Ptolemy Keraunos could not acquire in a short time. Hoping that the invasion of the Galatians would damage the independentist plans of the Thracian tribes, Ptolemy did nothing to stop the Celtic advance. Receiving no help from their new king, the Thracians decided to ally themselves with the newcomers and abandoned Ptolemy Keraunos. In the spring of 279 BC, the Galatians invaded Macedonia and clashed with Ptolemy Keraunos in a large pitched battle: the usurper was defeated and killed, leading to the rapid collapse of his kingdom. Macedonia remained in a state of complete political chaos for two years, while the Thracian tribes again became fully independent. Meanwhile, the march of the Galatians continued south, towards Greece. During 279 and 278 they raided the Greek countryside, before being stopped at the pass of Thermopylae by the military forces of Antigonus Gonatas. The Celts, however, were able to turn the strategic pass without fighting against the superior forces confronting them, and thus continued their advance towards southern Greece. Even Delphi and its famous sanctuary were raided by the Galatians, who

Thorakites with
Attic–Boeotian
helmet and scale
armour. (*Photo
and copyright by
Hetairoi*)

seemed unable to be stopped. Due to bad weather conditions, however, they were finally obliged to abandon Greece after having raided several locations.

While all these events took place in Greece, another group of Galatians from the Balkans invaded Thrace and then crossed the Hellespont into Asia. The massive presence of the Celts in Thrace was unacceptable for the Greeks, who feared another invasion and could not live with such a terrible menace on their borders. As a result, Antigonus Gonatas marched against the Galatians of Thrace with the intention of defeating them forever: he was able to achieve his objective, after which the son of Demetrius was considered as the new saviour of Greece. After two years of complete anarchy, Macedonia finally had a new king in the person of Antigonus Gonatas, who united his original possessions in Greece with Thrace and Macedonia. All Hellenistic Europe was in the hands of a single monarch, who initiated a new royal house. The Galatians who had already crossed the Hellespont continued their march across Anatolia. This region of Asia, which had been formerly part of Lysimachus' possessions, was now ruled as an independent kingdom by the dynasty of the Attalids. The latter had started to rule the city of Pergamon in 281 BC. The founder of this new royal house had been Philetaerus, an officer of Lysimachus. The small military forces of the Kingdom of Pergamon, however, could not defeat the Galatians, who were finally stopped only in 275 BC after being crushed by the large army of Antiochus, the master of Asia. After this defeat they remained in central Anatolia, where they continued to launch raids. Finally, in 232 BC, the Attalids defeated the Galatians again and forced them to settle and form their own independent kingdom (formally a vassal state of the Kingdom of Pergamon). In 275, more or less fifty years after Alexander the Great's death, the Hellenistic world had finally found a stable political organization: Hellenistic Europe was ruled by the Antigonids of Macedonia; Hellenistic Egypt remained under the firm control of the Ptolemies; Asia, with the exception of Pergamon, was the realm of the Seleucids. These three kingdoms, real superpowers of the ancient world, would be defeated only by the later incredible ascendancy of Rome.

Thorakites with spear and oval shield.
(*Photo and copyright by Hetairoi*)

Psilos with Pilos helmet and 'pelte' shield. (*Photo and copyright by Hetairoi*)

Psilos with
Thessalian 'petasos'
cap (a sun hat of
Thessalian origin
with broad and
floppy brim) and a
couple of javelins.
(*Photo and copyright
by Hetairoi*)

Psilos with Pilos cap and Thracian 'pelte'
shield. Note the use of a Thessalian mantle.
(*Photo and copyright by Hetairoi*)

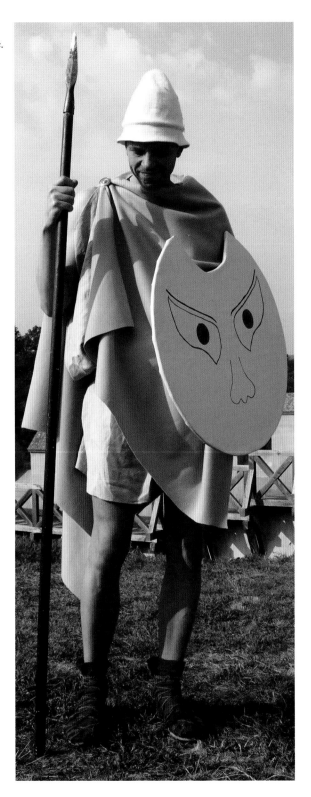

Chapter 5

The Armies of the Early Successors

After Alexander the Great's death, the Macedonian Army in Asia initially remained united under the command of the regent Perdiccas. It is important to note, however, that Alexander had left control of Macedonia and Greece in the hands of Antipater, who ruled both countries on behalf of the king. In order to face the eventual revolts of the Greeks or attacks by the Balkan tribes, Alexander had left Antipater a large number of soldiers, all Macedonians: 13,000 infantrymen and 1,600 cavalrymen. Presumably the 13,000 foot troops consisted of eight regiments (*taxeis*) of heavy infantrymen (with 1,500 men each), plus 1,000 light infantrymen (two companies of 500 soldiers each). The cavalry consisted of eight *ilai* (squadrons), with 200 men each. As is clear from these numbers, Antipater could count on a very large army: from the qualitative point of view, however, this was not comparable to the larger Army of Asia commanded by Perdiccas. It seems that the troops controlled by Antipater were reserve ones, specifically raised to garrison Macedonia and Greece after the departure of the regular forces ('foot companions' and 'horse companions'). When the Greek cities rose in open revolt, with the outbreak of the Lamian War, the army of Antipater had many difficulties in putting down the rebellion and was saved only by the arrival of Craterus' reinforcements taken from the Army of Asia. The latter consisted of 12,500 men: 6,000 veteran Macedonian phalangists, 4,000 infantry recruits from the newly conquered provinces (maybe *Epigoni*), 1,000 Asian light infantrymen (archers and slingers) and 1,500 cavalrymen. With the outbreak of the First War of the Diadochi, the unity of the Macedonian Army was finally destroyed: in this chapter we will try to describe the composition of the early Successors' armies, according to the few resources that we have from our primary sources. The early military forces of Ptolemy and Seleucus will be covered in two dedicated chapters, dealing with the armies of the Ptolemies and Seleucids.

As we have seen, the First War of the Diadochi was fought by Perdiccas and his ally Eumenes against a large coalition formed by Antipater, Craterus, Antigonus Monophtalmus, Ptolemy and Lysimachus. Eumenes (former secretary of Alexander the Great) became governor of Cappadocia in 322 BC, after Perdiccas finally conquered that last bastion of Persian resistance. Eumenes had no military experience to speak of, but when hostilities began between his master, Perdiccas, and Antipater he was able

Archer with Pilos cap. (*Photo and copyright by Hetairoi*)

to raise a large army from Anatolia. Against all odds, he was soon beloved by most of his new troops: this was not easy to achieve, especially because Eumenes was a Greek from the Thracian coast and not a 'pure' Macedonian. Yet he was soon able to gain the respect of the Macedonian veterans under his command. In total, his army included 26,000 soldiers: 20,000 infantrymen (a nucleus of Macedonian veterans from the garrisons of Anatolia plus a large number of new Asiatic recruits) and 6,000 cavalrymen (mostly excellent Cappadocian mounted skirmishers plus a certain number of Greek and Thracian horsemen). This excellent army was able to defeat the veteran military forces of Craterus, remnants of which passed into the service of Eumenes. When the Second War of the Diadochi began, Eumenes sided with the new regent, Polyperchon, against the powerful alliance formed by Cassander, Ptolemy and Antigonus. His main enemy was Antigonus, who had received control over Anatolia according to the peace agreement that followed the end of the previous war. In the first phase of the campaign Eumenes was abandoned by his cavalry commander, who deserted at the head of the Cappadocian cavalry. As a result, Eumenes' forces were besieged in Mora by those of Antigonus and reduced themselves to just a few hundred men. After escaping from Mora, Eumenes was able to raise a new – albeit much smaller – army to face Antigonus: this comprised 2,000 infantrymen (veteran Macedonians from his previous army) and 1,000 cavalrymen (Cappadocians who had remained loyal to him). These small forces were later augmented by the arrival of reinforcements sent to Eumenes by Polyperchon: the 3,000 elite veterans of the 'Regiment of the Royal Hypaspists'. The majority of these soldiers were aged at least 60, but no military unit of the Hellenistic world was comparable to them in terms of quality and experience. With the progress of time, the losses of this unit had been covered by absorbing veterans from the 'foot companions'. In addition to the Hypaspists, Polyperchon sent to Eumenes a large amount of money, with which the latter was able to recruit several thousand mercenaries (5,000 in total, from Anatolia, Syria and Cyprus). At this point Eumenes made a very intelligent move and marched towards the heart of Asia, in order to gain the support of most of the local satraps. After the agreements of Susa, the Asian governors sent a total of 24,000 infantrymen and 5,000 cavalry. The foot troops comprised 6,000 Asians armed in Macedonian fashion like phalangists (*Epigoni*) and 18,000 light skirmishers (mostly Asians from the eastern satrapies plus some mercenaries). The 5,000 cavalry included 1,000 Macedonian/Greek settlers who now lived in the eastern satrapies, 500 Thracian light horsemen recruited from the Thracian settlers and 3,500 Asian mounted skirmishers. The original nucleus of Eumenes' cavalry had been augmented from 1,000 to 1,200 men: these were organized into a Royal Squadron (*agema*) of 400 soldiers plus four normal squadrons (*ilai*) with 200 men each. Eumenes had decided to form his own mounted guard exactly like a legitimate Macedonian monarch: this

Detail of the personal equipment carried by an archer. (*Photo and copyright by Hetairoi*)

was formed of 300 loyal Cappadocians and 100 of his personal retainers (probably young aristocrats). The other 800 heavy horsemen were Macedonian veterans from the 'horse companions', who had decided to serve under Eumenes after the latter's arrival in Asia. During the decisive battle against Antigonus, Eumenes was abandoned by one of his eastern allies, and these Hypaspists changed sides. When the clash was over, Eumenes' army was no longer in existence: the Hypaspists, now in the service of Antigonus, were considered as too 'turbulent' and dangerous by their new commander, and thus were sent to serve as garrison troops to distant Arachosia. The local governor received a secret order from Antigonus, according to which it was decided to use the old Hypaspists in hazardous missions that would result in their death. Antigonus wanted to avoid any trouble and did everything possible to prevent the veteran Hypaspists from returning to Macedonia.

Polyperchon, Eumenes' main ally, was nominated by Antipater to succeed him as regent in 319 BC. After Antipater's death, however, the military forces in Macedonia and Greece refused to accept Polyperchon as regent and sided with Cassander (Antipater's son) in his rebellion. To face Cassander, Polyperchon was able to raise an army of 25,000 men: 20,000 Macedonian infantrymen (a hasty levy), 4,000 Greek infantrymen from allied cities and 1,000 Macedonian cavalrymen. He could also count on sixty-five war elephants, the survivors of the seventy brought to Europe from Babylon by Antipater in 317. As we have seen, however, Polyperchon was defeated by Cassander and confined to the Peloponnese area. Cassander initiated his revolt at the head of just 4,000 Greek mercenaries, but was later able to install a puppet regime in Athens and gain the loyalty of his father's military forces. At the zenith of his power, he could raise a total of 30,000 infantrymen and 2,000 cavalrymen: the majority of these were Macedonians, but Greek mercenaries continued to be a fundamental element of Cassander's army until his death.

Antigonus Monophtalmus began his incredible political career as governor of Phrygia. When he clashed for the first time with Eumenes, in 320 BC, he was in command of an army comprising 12,000 men and thirty war elephants. The infantry consisted of 10,000 soldiers, 5,000 of whom were veteran Macedonians while the others were local Asian troops, mostly from Phrygia. The cavalry was probably composed of 1,000 Macedonians (ex-members of the 'horse companions') and 1,000 mounted skirmishers from Phrygia. When Antigonus faced Eumenes again in 317, his army had seen gradual but constant numerical expansion, and he could now field a total of 28,000 infantrymen, 11,000 cavalry and sixty-five war elephants. The foot troops were formed by 8,000 Macedonian veteran phalangists, 9,000 mercenaries (several of them equipped as traditional peltasts), 8,000 Asians equipped in Macedonian fashion (Epigoni) and 3,000 loyal Phrygians (armed as peltasts). The heavy cavalry numbered 4,600 men:

Slinger with 'petasos' cap made of straw. (*Photo and copyright by Hetairoi*)

400 soldiers of the Royal Squadron (the mounted guard of Antigonus, formed by his personal retainers), 1,000 Macedonian veterans (five squadrons of former 'horse companions'), 1,000 Greek allies/mercenaries and 2,200 Macedonian/Greek settlers from the provinces of Asia. The light cavalry numbered 6,400 men: 1,000 Thracians, 600 assorted mercenaries, 2,500 Asian mounted skirmishers and 2,300 mercenaries from Taras in southern Italy. In 312 BC, Antigonus sent his son, Demetrius, to invade Egypt at the head of a large army comprising 12,500 infantrymen, 4,600 cavalrymen and forty-three war elephants. The foot troops included 2,000 veteran Macedonians, 1,000 loyal Phrygians, 8,000 mercenaries and 1,500 light infantry skirmishers; the cavalry was made up of Demetrius' personal *agema* of 200 retainers, 800 veteran Macedonians (in four squadrons), 300 Asian heavy cavalrymen, 100 Tarantine mercenary light horsemen and 3,000 Asian mounted skirmishers. After the death of his father, Demetrius was reduced to a sort of freebooter, being in command only of mercenaries and pirates. For example, he conducted his last military campaign, against Lysimachus and Seleucus in Anatolia, at the head of just 11,000 mercenaries.

Finally, some words on the military forces of Lysimachus, who had been nominated governor of Thrace by Alexander the Great and thus ruled Macedonian Europe together with Antipater while Alexander was completing his conquests in Asia. Initially he just commanded a small army of 4,000 infantrymen and 2,000 cavalrymen, mostly Macedonians or Greek mercenaries who formed the garrison of Thrace. During the following decades, however, Lysimachus was able to vastly increase the number of his military forces; by 301 BC, he had an army of 44,000 infantrymen and 3,000 cavalrymen. Lysimachus generally preferred to avoid using the tribal contingents of the Thracians, so as not to cause the outbreak of internal revolts. Since he could not count on consistent numbers of Macedonians, he mostly relied on mercenaries: these were frequently Illyrians, but also Greeks from the cities located on the Thracian coast. Over time, however, the master of Thrace also started to enlist a number of Thracian tribal warriors, the status of whom was that of allies and not of subjects. Apparently, a number of these Thracians were trained and equipped in Macedonian fashion in order to be employed as phalangists. After defeating Antigonus Monophtalmus, Lysimachus added Anatolia to his personal possessions. As a result, he was able to start recruiting local contingents of Asian troops (mostly light infantry). After Lysimachus' death, the military forces described above passed under the command of Ptolemy Keraunos, who soon had to face the massive and destructive invasion of the Galatians. After being abandoned by the Thracians, the usurper was crushed with his remaining forces by the Celtic hordes.

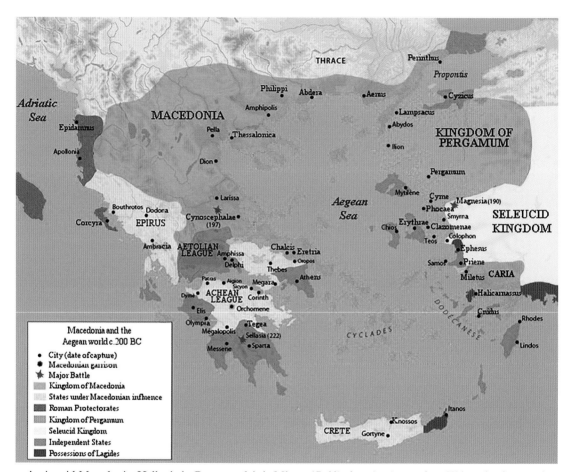

Antigonid Macedonia, Hellenistic Greece and Asia Minor. (*Public domain pictures from Wikimedia Commons*)

Chapter 6

The Antigonid Army

When Antigonus Gonatas became King of Macedonia after the Galatian invasions, he was initially very reluctant to rebuild the national Macedonian army: his new kingdom was just emerging from a long period of internal unrest and the human resources of the territory had been deeply affected by the many wars fought on Macedonian territory since Alexander the Great's death. Many thousands of men had gone to Asia to fight and had decided to remain there as settlers or been killed during the various military campaigns. The troops used by Antigonus Gonatas to defeat the Galatians were mostly Greek mercenaries, who were extremely loyal to their leader. During the first years of his rule over Macedonia, Antigonus preferred to continue using Greek mercenaries, and thus increased their numbers. In addition, he recruited large numbers of Galatians as mercenaries and included them in his army: after having been defeated, these fierce Celtic warriors were now in search of employment. By the end of Antigonus' reign, around 240 BC, recruiting of native Macedonians had again became very common and thus a real Macedonian Army had been effectively re-formed. In general, if compared with the armies of other Hellenistic states, that of Antigonid Macedonia had two main distinctive features: a lack of war elephants and the relatively minor importance given to cavalry. Antigonus Gonatas apparently had just twenty war elephants in his army, inherited from Alexander the Great and arriving to him after service under several rulers (Antipater, Cassander, Lysimachus and Ptolemy Keraunos). Unlike the Ptolemies and Seleucids, who could count on the African or Asian elephants from their territories, the Antigonids had to import war elephants from other states. Since these war beasts were considered the most lethal weapon of the Hellenistic armies, it was very difficult for the Macedonians to obtain them from a potential rival state like Egypt or the Seleucid Empire. Antigonid Macedonia continued to have excellent heavy cavalry, like in the days of Alexander the Great, but generally lacked large light cavalry forces. As we will see in the following chapters, the armies of the other Hellenistic states included thousands of light horsemen equipped as mounted skirmishers or archers. This was not the case with Macedonia, where the influence of Persian military traditions based on light cavalry troops was insignificant.

'Horse companion' with Attic helmet and leather muscle cuirass. (*Photo and copyright by Hetairoi*)

The real core of the Antigonid Army was represented by the elite heavy infantry of the phalanx, which was considered the best infantry of all the Hellenistic armies. Differently from the Ptolemies and Seleucids, the Antigonids could recruit their phalangists from the native population of Macedonia: the foot soldiers of the Antigonid Army were the direct heirs of Alexander the Great's phalangists and had thus inherited most of their ancestors' military traditions. The phalanxes of the Ptolemies and Seleucids, instead, had to be recruited from the small communities of Macedonian or Greek settlers living in Egypt and Asia. These military settlers, known as *kleruchs*, were the descendants of the Macedonian and Greek soldiers who had survived the campaigns of Alexander the Great and had decided to settle down in the newly conquered areas of the Macedonian Empire. In exchange for military service, they received some land and thus could live as soldiers/farmers. Compared with the rest of the native population, however, the *kleruchs* were a small minority; in addition, as time progressed, the original veterans of Alexander started to disappear and were only partly replaced by their direct heirs. This was a great problem for the Ptolemies and Seleucids, since it had been impossible to train the local African and Asian levies of their new kingdoms in the usual tactics of the phalanx. This was absolutely not the case for Antigonid Macedonia, where the monarchy could always count on the excellent manpower provided by the local farmers and shepherds. Several decades of wars fought on Macedonian territory had obviously diminished the demographic capabilities of the region, but with the progress of time and the creation of a new, stable monarchy the population of Macedonia started to grow again. Unlike the *kleruchs*, the Antigonid phalangists were of pure Macedonian blood, which was important for the ideology of the time.

The Antigonid heavy infantrymen were organized into three large divisions, or *strategiai*, each commanded by an important high officer known as a *strategos*. The first division was that of the *Peltastoi*, followed by those of the *Chalkaspides* and *Leukaspides*. More or less each of these three divisions included 5,000 phalangists, so the total of heavy infantrymen in the Antigonid Army was roughly 15,000. Every free and able-bodied Macedonian man was expected to serve in the royal army from the age of 20, and the infantry divisions were divided according to the age of their members. Each division was structured on five battalions or *chiliarchies* of 1,000 men, commanded by a *hegemon*. Each battalion was formed of four *speirai* (basic phalanxes) of 256 soldiers each, divided into four companies known as *tetrarchiai* and including 64 men. The single *tetrarchiai* were structured, as usual, on four files of sixteen men each (a *dekas*). The *Peltastoi* were considered the real elite of the Macedonian Army; their name can easily be translated as 'peltasts', but it is important not to confuse them with the category of light infantrymen inspired by Thracian and Illyrian military fashion. As

'Horse companion' with Attic helmet. (*Photo and copyright by Hetairoi*)

we have seen, since the time of Philip of Macedon the Greek word *pelte* had started to indicate the new small round shield employed by the Macedonian heavy infantrymen: it is in this sense that we could now use the term *Peltastoi* for the Antigonid Army, in order to indicate the elite phalangists. The *Peltastoi* were the elite division of the Macedonian Army: it was composed of the best and youngest men of Macedonia, who were conscripted to serve in the *Peltastoi* division for a limited period of time. After reaching the age of 35, they returned to their civilian life or enlisted in one of the two 'reserve' divisions (the *Chalkaspides* and *Leukaspides*, formed of older men). While the other two divisions were only mobilized in case of war, the *Peltastoi* were always ready to fight. In addition, while the two 'reserve' divisions were mostly intended for service on Macedonian national territory, the *Peltastoi* could also be employed outside the borders of Macedonia. In many aspects, the *Peltastoi* were the direct heirs of Alexander the Great's Hypaspists. They fought as phalangists but wore no armour, which gave them a superior level of mobility. This made the *Peltastoi* perfectly suited to conduct 'special operations'; like the former Hypaspists, they are mentioned on several occasions as being employed as a link between the phalanx and other categories of troops (cavalry or light infantry).

The 5,000 *Peltastoi* were divided into two main groups: the *Agema* (formed by the first two battalions) and that of the ordinary *Peltastoi* (the remaining three battalions). The Greek word *Agema*, as we have seen, means 'vanguard', which clearly indicates that its members were an 'elite within an elite'. Members of the *Agema* were also known as the *Nicatores* (the 'Conquerors'). Like the former vanguard battalion of the Hypaspists, these 2,000 elite soldiers were chosen from the whole Macedonian Army for their personal strength, vigour and experience. Apparently, members of the *Agema* battalions were senior *Peltastoi* who had already served for several years. Normal *Peltastoi* were to serve until the age of 35; members of the *Agema* were former normal *Peltastoi* who continued to serve for another period of ten years (thus reaching the age of 45). The *Agema* acted as the foot guard of the Macedonian kings and generally performed extremely well during pitched battles. The two 'reserve' divisions of the Macedonian heavy infantry, the *Chalkaspides* and Leukaspides, could be translated respectively as the 'bronze shields' and 'white shields', since both units took their names from the colour of their shields (similarly to Alexander the Great's *Argyraspides*). Generally speaking, both divisions had the same internal organization described above (with five battalions each). The *Chalkaspides* were an active reserve, which could also be employed – if needed – outside the Macedonian borders; the *Leukaspides*, however, were a static reserve that could be used only inside Macedonia to face military emergencies (like a foreign invasion). Members of the *Chalkaspides* were mostly aged between 35 and 45, since the majority of them had already served in the

Macedonian light cavalryman with
'kausia' cap (a flat hat of Macedonian
origin which was very popular during
the Hellenistic period) and heavy
cloak. (*Photo and copyright by Hetairoi*)

Peltastoi. Apparently, however, the *Chalkaspides* also included younger soldiers who had not been selected for service in the elite *Peltastoi*. The *Leukaspides* were all skilled veterans, a sort of national reserve formed by experienced soldiers who had already served in the *Chalkaspides* and who had passed the age of 45.

After the collapse of Alexander the Great's empire, the elite cavalry of the 'horse companions' remained in Asia and later became part of the Seleucid Army. The new Antigonid Army of Macedonia thus had to form entirely new units of heavy cavalry. If replacing the original 'foot companions' was quite simple thanks to the excellent manpower available in Macedonia, the same could not be said for the 'horse companions': most of the Macedonian aristocrats who formed the original heavy cavalry had died during the long campaigns against the Persian Empire or had definitively transferred to Asia. When Antigonus Gonatas assumed power, there were just a few hundred Macedonians who were rich enough to serve as heavy cavalrymen. During the following decades, the number of Macedonian cavalry squadrons varied according to circumstances, but never reached the high establishments that existed under Philip of Macedon or Alexander the Great. The Macedonian heavy cavalry comprised just 300 men; in 171 BC, at the outbreak of the Third Macedonian War between the Antigonids and Rome, the Macedonian cavalry reached its highest establishment (3,000 men) since the days of Alexander. As a consequence of these fluctuating numbers, the structure of the Macedonian cavalry was not very stable during this period: what we know for sure is that there was always an elite Sacred Squadron (*hiera ile*), which was the direct heir of the former *basilike ile* (Royal Squadron). Apparently this unit was the first to be re-formed after the ascendancy of the new Antigonid royal house, having an initial establishment of 300 soldiers. Later, this Sacred Squadron was increased to 400 men, reaching the same establishment of the former Royal Squadron. The *hiera ile* was the only stable unit of the Macedonian heavy cavalry, acting as mounted guard for the Antigonid kings. All the other units were formed according to military necessities and could be easily disbanded. Regarding organization, we should point out that the Macedonian heavy cavalry was still structured on *ilai* (squadrons) of 200 men each. The various squadrons were commanded by officers known as *ilarchai*. For the campaign of 171 BC, for example, the Macedonian cavalry was able to deploy the following units: 400 soldiers of the Sacred Squadron and 2,600 'standard' cavalrymen in thirteen squadrons of 200 men each.

As under Philip of Macedon and Alexander the Great, the Macedonian Army continued to comprise allied and mercenary contingents made up by foreign warriors during the Antigonid period. As we have seen, Antigonus Gonatas used large numbers of Galatian mercenaries at the beginning of his reign, but over time the use of Celtic warriors steadily diminished. We continue to find Galatians in the Macedonian

Thessalian light cavalryman with 'petasos' cap and Thracian boots. (*Photo and copyright by Hetairoi*)

Army for most of the period under investigation, but their numbers never exceeded 2,000. Thracians were employed in large numbers, both as mercenaries and as allies: they were mostly equipped as light infantrymen but sometimes could also serve as cavalrymen. The Illyrians, as in previous periods, continued to provide excellent troops of light infantry skirmishers (javelineers and slingers): Paeonians and Agrianes were still the major contributors among the various tribes, sending contingents that usually numbered between 1,000 and 3,000 men. The allied Illyrian tribes from the central Balkans also sent large auxiliary contingents, especially when foreign invasions menaced Macedonia. Greeks continued to be the main source of mercenary/allied soldiers, particularly during the early period of Antigonus Gonatas. Generally speaking, the Antigonid monarchs always tried to preserve as much as possible their precious Macedonian soldiers, preferring to employ mercenaries to perform dangerous tasks or secondary duties like garrisoning fortresses or cities. Some of the Greek mercenaries were cavalrymen, but the majority were equipped as infantry. Cretan archers, as always considered to be the best of all Greek mercenaries, continued to be employed in large numbers under the Antigonids.

It is important to note that by the end of Antigonus Gonata's long reign, most of the Greek mercenary/allied infantrymen were no longer equipped as hoplites or Thracian-type peltasts, but as *thureophoroi*. The Galatian invasions had obliged the Hellenistic armies to face a new kind of enemy: the Celtic warrior, who had the offensive weapons of a light infantryman but at the same time carried a large defensive shield. The Hellenistic commanders, influenced by their new enemies, soon copied the Galatian personal equipment and created a new category of soldiers known as *thureophoroi*. Basically, a *thureophoros* was a medium infantryman, a new version of the traditional Thracian-type peltast; his name derived from the *thureos* shield, a Greek copy of the usual Celtic oval shield (with metal strip boss and central spine). Each *thureophoros* also carried a sword, a long thrusting spear and two javelins. Armour was not used, but each soldier generally had a helmet. Apparently the Celtic oval shield had already been adopted by the Illyrians and Thracians before the Greeks, so most of the mercenary/allied infantrymen sent to Macedonia by these two peoples were a sort of *thureophoroi*. In general terms, the *thureophoros* operated in an intermediate role between the heavy infantry phalangist and the light infantry skirmisher: the *thureophoroi* could support the light infantry thanks to their large shields but could also deploy themselves in phalanx formation thanks to their thrusting spears. Apparently this new category of soldier was perfectly suited to the military needs of the smaller Hellenistic states, and thanks to their great mobility over every kind of terrain, the *thureophoroi* were frequently used as border troops. Their tactical flexibility and adaptability were much appreciated by the Greek cities, with the result that most of the Greek hoplites or peltasts soon started to be re-equipped with the oval *thureos*.

Basic Hellenistic dress with 'kausia'
cap and long-sleeved tunic. (*Photo and
copyright by Hetairoi*)

Chapter 7

The Ptolemaic Army

When Ptolemy became satrap of Egypt after the 'Partition of Babylon', the military forces under his command were quite scarce, in practice consisting of the small garrison left in the country by Alexander the Great which was made up of a few Macedonians and mercenaries. Ptolemy arrived in his new country with no soldiers and no treasure, but he was soon involved in large wars against the other Diadochi. In order to build up an efficient military force in a very short time, he was obliged to use the riches of Egypt to hire great numbers of mercenaries. Ptolemy initially preferred to not recruit Egyptians, to prevent the outbreak of popular revolts: Egypt had been the last important conquest of the Persians and thus the country still had a recent tradition of self-rule. When Perdiccas invaded Egypt during the First War of the Diadochi, Ptolemy could field only an army of mercenaries against the veteran troops of the central Macedonian Army of Asia. Thanks to the assassination of Perdiccas, however, Ptolemy was able to stop the invasion and finally establish himself as an independent monarch. The failed attack of Perdiccas against Egypt was a real turning point for the military forces of the Ptolemies: after the murder of the ambitious regent, many Macedonian soldiers (veterans of Asia who had served under Alexander the Great) decided to remain in Egypt to serve under the new local royal house. They soon formed military colonies of *kleruchs* (settlers), which became the backbone of the new Ptolemaic Army.

Each military settler was given a grant of land (*kleros*), which varied according to his rank and arm of service. He would have lived and worked on his farm during peacetime, being called up for military service only in time of war. Ptolemy did everything possible to make this system work, especially when the original nucleus of veteran Macedonians started to disappear: he later transformed several mercenaries and prisoners of war from other Hellenistic armies into military settlers. In 312 BC, the new army of Ptolemy was able to defeat Demetrius at the Battle of Gaza. The victory of Egypt over the military forces of Asia resulted in a general increase of the Ptolemies' military capabilities. Ptolemy was able to capture forty-three war elephants from the army of Demetrius, and absorbed into his forces 8,000 prisoners of war (all phalangists, Macedonians or Greek mercenaries). These prisoners of war were soon transformed into *kleruchs*. The majority of the *kleroi* farms were located in Lower

Basic Hellenistic dress with 'kausia' cap and short–sleeved tunic. (*Photo and copyright by Hetairoi*)

Egypt, particularly in the Nile Delta region, the result of an intelligent strategic choice made by Ptolemy, who decided to place most of his military colonists in the area of Egypt that was most exposed to foreign invasions by sea. The Nile Delta was also very important for the economy of Egypt: the most fertile lands of the country were located there, with their vital production of grain. For the training of these military settlers' sons, the Ptolemies even created a sort of cadet corps, whose members were known as *Epigoni* and received specific military training in order to be able to replace their fathers once they became too old. The *kleruchs* soon became the core of the new Ptolemaic Army, providing the manpower needed for the phalanxes and heavy cavalry. The use of mercenaries generally decreased, but never disappeared until the fall of Hellenistic Egypt. In later times, Egypt had no more opportunities to absorb large numbers of Macedonian prisoners of war: as a result, since money was not a problem for the richest of all the Hellenistic states, mercenaries again became the most important component of the Ptolemaic Army (especially during the last period of its history). Similarly to the Seleucid Army, the Ptolemaic Army included three main categories of troops: the 'regular' forces of the Royal Guard (a permanent body of professional soldiers stationed around the Egyptian capital of Alexandria), the 'reserve' forces of the Macedonian/Greek military settlers (*kleruchs*) and the mercenaries. The soldiers of the Royal Guard were all Macedonian military colonists, since Ptolemy had started to build up his 'regular' army after the defeat of Perdiccas. As a result, at least initially, most of these soldiers were veterans of Alexander the Great's campaigns.

The Royal Guard included a total of 5,700 men, organized into three elite regiments: the heavy cavalry of the 'horse companions' (with 700 soldiers), the chosen infantry of the *Basilikon Agema* (3,000 men) and the heavy infantry of the Peltasts (2,000 soldiers). The heavy cavalry regiment was probably structured on two squadrons: a Royal Squadron with 400 men (acting as mounted guard of the king) and another squadron of 300 men (a mounted guard for the heir to the throne). We can find something similar in the army of Antigonus Monophtalmus, which included a Royal Squadron of 400 soldiers protecting the king and another of 300 soldiers protecting Demetrius. The *Basilikon Agema* was clearly the Ptolemaic version of the Macedonian Hypaspists and thus was presumably organized into six battalions (*lochoi*) with 500 soldiers each. Regarding the 2,000 Peltasts, it seems clear that they were the Egyptian equivalent of the Antigonid *Peltastoi*: elite heavy infantrymen (phalangists) chosen from the whole army for their great personal capabilities. Until the outbreak of the Fourth Syrian War against the Seleucids in 219 BC, the structure of the Ptolemaic Royal Guard remained unchanged: in that year, however, Egypt faced a serious military emergency that led to a real revolution in the military forces of the Ptolemies.

When Antiochus III, ruler of the Seleucid Empire from 233 BC, invaded Egypt with a very large army, the Ptolemies, due to the scarce number of their Macedonian

Basic Hellenistic dress with 'kausia' cap
and Doric chiton. (*Photo and copyright by
Hetairoi*)

forces and with the possibility of a definitive Seleucid victory, were obliged for the first time to recruit local Egyptians in their army in order to repulse the foreign attack. With the Persian conquest of Egypt in 525 BC, the traditional local warrior caste that had defended the pharaohs for centuries had been officially suppressed. Until the arrival of the Achaemenids, the army of Egypt had been formed by a closed caste of warriors, forbidden to practice other activities outside of combat and provided with grants of tax-free land as a reward for their military services. The profession of soldier was hereditary in Egypt, like in many other countries at the time; it was also strongly linked to several symbolic and religious meanings. In spite of the suppression ordered by the Persians, the Egyptian warrior caste continued to exist under the Achaemenids: Egyptian soldiers formed a minor but efficient part of the Persian military forces. Obliged by the circumstances to rely on his subjects, the Ptolemaic monarch of 219 BC, Ptolemy IV, recruited a large number of native Egyptians to fight against the Seleucids. Some 20,000 Egyptians were added to the army, being trained and equipped as phalangists. As a result, the original phalanx of 25,000 Macedonian *kleruchs* was joined by a second phalanx formed by the new native recruits. The inclusion of these new local soldiers, known as *machimoi*, in the Ptolemaic Army soon proved to be a wise decision, as Ptolemy IV was able to decisively defeat Antiochus III at the Battle of Raphia in 217 BC. The recruiting of Egyptian *machimoi* also had consequences for the organization of the Ptolemaic Royal Guard: after the victory of Raphia, an elite unit of native Egyptians was included in the Guard. This was the new regiment of the *Machimoi Epilektoi* (Chosen Machimoi), which was formed with chosen soldiers taken from the 20,000 Egyptian phalangists who fought with honour at Raphia. We have no idea of their numbers, but it is highly probable that they were 2,000 like their Macedonian equivalent (the Peltasts). The inclusion of the *machimoi* in the Ptolemaic Army led to a general revival of ethnic Egyptian political involvement. After Raphia, the political issues of the native Egyptians could no longer be ignored by the Ptolemies, and the *machimoi* became an important power that the foreign royal house had to consider. Macedonian control over Egypt had relied more on the apathy of the locals than on their loyalty, but after receiving the same training and weapons as the Macedonians, the Egyptians soon started to agitate for greater equality. The social pressure of the native Egyptians led to the outbreak of several uprisings: in 205 BC, the locals finally rose up in open revolt against the Ptolemies, in what is commonly known as the 'Egyptian Revolt'. For several years the rebels were even able to form a secessionist Kingdom of Upper Egypt, led by a native pharaoh. The revolt was suppressed only in 183 BC, after many years of cruel civil war.

The Macedonian 'reserve' phalanx of the *kleruchs* included a total of 25,000 men; these were organized into five large divisions, or *strategiai*, each commanded by an

Panoply of a phalangist. (*Photo and copyright by Hetairoi*)

important high officer known as a *strategos* and including 5,000 soldiers. Each division was structured on five battalions, or *chiliarchies*, of 1,000 men, commanded by a *chiliarchos*. Each battalion was formed by four *syntagmata* (basic phalanxes) of 256 soldiers each, divided into two companies known as *hekatontarchies* and including 128 men. Each company was divided into two smaller units of sixty-four men called *pentekontarchies*. The single *pentekontarchies* were structured, as usual, on four files of sixteen men each (called *dekas*). The Egyptian *machimoi* phalangists enlisted in the Ptolemaic Army regardless of social class, since the profession of soldier was no longer hereditary as in previous centuries. However, they continued to receive a grant of tax-free land in exchange for their military services. The *machimoi* phalanx was structured exactly like the Macedonian one, with its 20,000 soldiers organized into four large divisions of 5,000 men each; the only difference was in the denomination of the battalions, which were known as *laarchiai*.

Regarding cavalry, its core was formed by the heavy squadrons provided by the *kleruchs* military settlers. Egypt did not have a great tradition of mounted troops, and thus the first Ptolemies had to rely only on Macedonians and mercenaries to deploy a good cavalry force. The Macedonian 'reserve' cavalry was organized into regiments known as *hipparchiai*, each of which included 500 men and was commanded by an officer (*hipparchos*). Each regiment was divided into five squadrons (*lochoi*) of 100 soldiers, which were in turn divided into ten *dekas*. In total there were five regiments of Macedonian cavalry, deploying 2,500 heavy horsemen. The light cavalry was provided by mercenaries who had been recruited by Ptolemy during the first phase of his reign and who had later settled as military colonists around the Nile Delta. These were organized into four regiments, each having a different ethnic composition: the first was made of Thessalians, the second of Thracians, the third of Mysians and the last of Persians. Since these light horsemen were not Macedonians anddid not serve as elite heavy cavalry, they received a different treatment from their *kleruchs* equivalent: while each Macedonian horseman received 100 acres of land, the ex-mercenaries were given just 70 acres. The original mercenaries who had formed these four regiments gradually disappeared over time: as a result, the ethnic peculiarities of each light regiment were abandoned and the land given to each light horseman was increased to 80 acres. By the second century BC, the four light *hipparchiai* were no longer even named after their original ethnic composition. Unlike what happened with the infantry, native Egyptians were never included in the Ptolemaic cavalry in large numbers, mostly due to the lack of horses and cavalry traditions that characterized Egypt during this time.

As for war elephants, as we have already seen, Ptolemy captured forty-three from Demetrius at the Battle of Gaza and thus created the Ptolemaic elephant corps. After the death of these original pachyderms, however, the Ptolemies were prevented from acquiring new Indian elephants due to their long rivalry with the Seleucids (who controlled Asia and had a monopoly over war elephants). As a result, the Ptolemaic kings started to organize hunting expeditions in North Africa to capture local elephants: these, albeit being smaller than the Indian ones, were a good alternative to create a sizeable elephant corps. Several ports and hunting stations were established on the coasts of modern Eritrea and Somalia, creating a network around the commerce of African elephants. Once captured, the pachyderms were shipped down the Red Sea in specially designed boats. Apparently this system worked quite well, at least during the first decades: at Raphia, for example, the Ptolemaic Army was able to deploy seventy-three African war elephants.

Mercenaries were always a very important component of the Ptolemaic Army, especially at the beginning. It is important, however, to distinguish two different phases in their employment. During the reign of Ptolemy, large numbers of

Panoply of a phalangist. (*Photo and copyright by Hetairoi*)

Macedonian mercenaries were still available for service and thus could be easily recruited. With the formation of Antigonid Macedonia, however, it became almost impossible for the Ptolemies to hire significant contingents of 'pure' Macedonian professional soldiers. As a result, mercenaries of other nationalities started to be employed on a much larger scale than before. Mercenaries were generally used by the Ptolemies as garrison troops, particularly in Cyprus and the other temporary possessions of the Ptolemies located outside Egypt. Over the years, however, the majority of the garrisons located in Egypt also started to be composed of mercenaries. Greeks always remained the most numerous. At the Battle of Raphia, for example, there were 15,000 of them in the Ptolemaic Army: 8,000 heavy infantrymen (who fought as phalangists with the Macedonian *kleruch* phalanx), 2,000 traditional peltasts, 3,000 Cretan archers and 2,000 cavalrymen. In addition to the Cretan archers, the Ptolemies employed large numbers of Rhodian slingers, famed for their deadly skills and considered the best slingers in the world. However, as with the Antigonid Army, most of the Greek mercenaries in the service of the Ptolemies eventually transformed themselves from hoplites/peltasts into the new *thureophoroi*. The Ptolemies also recruited large numbers of *thureophoroi* from Anatolia: during this period, they always retained some temporary possessions on the coasts of

Thrace and Anatolia. From these military bases they could recruit large groups of mercenaries, which were then sent to Egypt or employed as garrison troops in local fortifications and cities. Mysians, Cilicians, Lycians and Pamphylians were the most appreciated, and all fought equipped as *thureophoroi*.

It is very interesting to note, however, that the *thureophoroi* did not represent the last stage in the long evolution of the Greek/Anatolian mercenaries' equipment. When the Romans started to fight against the Hellenistic states, particularly after their first victory over Macedonia in 197 BC, the Hellenistic commanders started to understand that the traditional phalanx was no match for the Roman legion. While the phalanx could operate effectively only on vast, flat terrains, the Roman legionaries could fight in every possible environment thanks to their great flexibility and adaptability. In addition, the personal equipment of the Roman legionaries was something totally new to the Hellenistic military world: each single legionary could be employed either as a light infantry skirmisher or heavy infantryman. Roman soldiers carried heavy javelins (*pila*) which enabled them to harass the enemy as light infantrymen; but they also had large oval shields and short swords (the *scutum* and *gladius*) that were perfect for hand-to-hand fighting in close formation. Finally, they wore armour made of chainmail: this, despite being quite heavy, was flexible enough to permit very rapid movements and gave a superior level of personal protection to each soldier (Roman chainmail – *lorica hamata* – was far superior to any kind of Hellenistic infantry armour). As the battles of the First Macedonian War clearly showed, the Roman legions were easily able to swarm around the flanks of a phalanx. This type of manoeuvre, which had never been realized before by any enemy facing the Hellenistic states, caused the quick disintegration of every phalanx. Since the early days of Philip and Alexander, it had been clear to Macedonian military commanders that the greatest weakness of the phalanxes was their exposed flanks: this was the main reason behind the creation of the Hypaspists. Now, since the latter had disappeared from Hellenistic military forces, the commanders of the various Hellenistic armies started to reform their troops to create a new category of soldiers that could protect the flanks of the phalanx and fight against the Roman legionaries on almost equal terms. To achieve this ambitious objective, the military leaders started to transform the *thureophoroi* into a Hellenistic version of the Roman legionaries. These new soldiers became known as *thorakitai* ('cuirassed soldiers') because they were equipped with chainmail armour like their Roman opponents. We could say that the *thorakitai* were *thureophoroi* with armour: the addition of chainmail transformed them into heavy infantrymen, who already carried the same kind of oval shield used by the Romans (who had copied it from the Celts like the *thureophoroi*). Deployed on the flanks of the phalanx, the *thorakitai* were sufficiently flexible and well equipped to confront the Roman legionaries either

Panoply of a Hypaspist. (*Photo and copyright by Hetairoi*)

in skirmish order or hand-to-hand combat. Unfortunately for the Hellenistic states, however, the reform of the *thorakitai* remained quite limited from a numerical point of view: the 'regular' armies of the various states continued to be made up of traditional phalangists and the new equipment of the *thorakitai* was adopted on a significant scale only by mercenary forces.

Other notable groups of mercenaries were those of the Thracians and Galatians; the former started to be employed in Egypt by Ptolemy, who later transformed a number of them into military settlers known as 'foreign kleruchs'. At the Battle of Raphia, for example, there were a total of 6,000 Thracians: 4,000 'foreign kleruchs' and 2,000 newly recruited mercenaries. Galatians started to be recruited from 274 BC; despite expectations, however, they proved to be undisciplined troops and never played a significant military role. Some of them were later transformed into 'foreign kleruchs' like the Thracians. Libyan mercenaries from North Africa were also quite common: apparently these were equipped as phalangists in Macedonian fashion like the Egyptian *machimoi*. At the Battle of Raphia there were 3,000 of these. The Ptolemies also employed a number of Jewish and Arab auxiliaries: these were not mercenaries, but a sort of frontier guards/policemen who were stationed on the land borders of Egypt. By the second century BC, policemen also received grants of land exactly like the *kleruchs* and thus transformed themselves into military settlers. Judging from the historical sources we have, the Jewish frontier guards were stationed on Egypt's southern border with Nubia, while the Arab ones (mostly Idumaeans) were used to garrison Egypt's desert border in the Sinai. These policemen had no proper military role, but since their farms were located on the borders of the kingdom they were to act as the first defensive line in case of a foreign invasion.

Finally, some words on the Roman mercenaries of the late Ptolemies. In 58 BC, Ptolemy XII did nothing to oppose the Roman occupation of Cyprus, which had been part of the Ptolemaic possessions since the times of the first Ptolemy. This clearly illustrated the political and military weakness of the Ptolemies to the Egyptian population, demonstrating that Egypt was in the process of becoming a vassal state of Rome. The population of the kingdom, in particular that of Alexandria, could not accept this situation and soon rose up in open revolt. Ptolemy XII, surprised by the events, fled in exile to Rome. During the three years he spent in Rome, the deposed king gradually gained support from the Roman Senate with the objective of returning to Egypt. In 55 BC, after difficult negotiations, the Romans finally decided to restore Ptolemy XII to his throne in order to have a 'puppet' king in Egypt. Aulus Gabinius, the Roman proconsul of Syria, marched to Egypt at the head of a Roman provincial army and restored Ptolemy XII after a brief campaign. Before returning to Syria, however, Gabinius decided to leave 2,500 of his men under the orders of the restored king. The country was still on the verge of revolt and these Roman soldiers would have protected Ptolemy from any possible rebellion. The Roman garrison of Egypt soon started to adopt the local manners and way of life, becoming completely alienated from the Roman Republic. After their integration into the Ptolemaic Army, these Roman soldiers transformed themselves into proper mercenaries and started to be known as *Gabiniani* (from the name of their former commander). The 2,500 *Gabiniani*, however, were not all Romans: 2,000 of them were proper Roman legionaries, while the remaining 500 were auxiliary cavalrymen from central Europe (Celts and Germans). Life in Alexandria was much better than the harsh Roman military discipline, and the *Gabiniani* soon became the strongest supporters of the Ptolemies. They married local women and created new families in Egypt; Ptolemy XII could always count on them, especially in case of internal revolts. When the king died in 51 BC, his oldest surviving children (Ptolemy XIII and Cleopatra VII) were supposed to rule jointly as husband and wife. Cleopatra, however, soon exiled her brother and started to rule alone, putting her in conflict with the *Gabiniani*, who had supported the ascendancy to the throne of Ptolemy XIII.

Phrygian helmet with leather muscle cuirass. (*Photo and copyright by Hetairoi*)

In 50 BC, the new Roman governor of Syria, Marcus Calpurnius Bibulus, sent his sons as envoys to Egypt with the objective of bringing the *Gabiniani* back into Roman service. Roman Syria was strongly menaced by the Parthians, who had defeated the Roman Army at Carrhae just three years before. As a result, Bibulus was assembling all the Roman forces available in the region to protect Syria. The *Gabiniani* refused to abandon Alexandria to fight against the Parthians and killed the two sons of Bibulus. Cleopatra, being in clear difficulty with Rome, ordered the arrest of the *Gabiniani* who had killed the Roman envoys and handed them over in chain to Bibulus. This event led to the revolt of the Roman mercenaries, who obliged Cleopatra to rule jointly with her brother Ptolemy (who returned from exile). In 49 BC, after the outbreak of the Roman civil war between Caesar and Pompey, the latter required military assistance from Egypt. Ptolemy and Cleopatra agreed to his requests and sent the 500 horsemen of the *Gabiniani* to Pompey. At the end of the year, however, civil war broke out again between the two siblings and Ptolemy was able to become the only ruler of Egypt thanks to the decisive support of his Roman mercenaries. After being defeated by Caesar at the Battle of Pharsalus, Pompey fled to Egypt and tried to gain the support of the Ptolemies. The Egyptian monarch, however, clearly understood that the power of Pompey was at its end and thus ordered his assassination (which was organized by two members of the *Gabiniani*). Caesar arrived in Egypt a few days after the murder of Pompey, but instead of being favourable to Ptolemy due to the elimination of his main rival, he sided with Cleopatra and supported her claims to the throne. At this point the troops of Caesar were involved in the local civil war, in what became known as the Alexandrinian War. The *Gabiniani* and the majority of the Ptolemaic military units fought against Cleopatra's supporters and Caesar's legionaries. The battle in Alexandria was brief but extremely cruel: while Caesar and Cleopatra were victorious, it seems that the *Gabiniani* fought with great valour before being defeated (judging from the words of Caesar). After the destruction of the *Gabiniani*, Caesar left three of his legions in Egypt to protect Cleopatra: the XXVII, XXVIII and XXIX. Later, when Mark Antony became the new lover of Cleopatra, a new royal bodyguard was formed with veteran Roman legionaries to protect the triumvir and queen.

To conclude, it is interesting to note that Egypt was not the only Hellenistic state located in North Africa. There was also the Greek city of Kyrene in Libya, that had been founded as a colony in 630 BC. Kyrene was practically abandoned by both the Persians and Alexander the Great, later being reconquered by Ptolemy. Since the establishment of the Ptolemaic Kingdom, however, the city remained tied very closely to Egypt. During the Hellenistic states period Kyrene was variously a province of Egypt, a client kingdom under a ruler from the Ptolemaic royal house or a fully independent city-state. Like every Greek city, Kyrene relied on a military force of citizens/hoplites. These,

Panoply of a *Psilos*. (*Photo and copyright by Hetairoi*)

however, were supplemented by a number of four-horse war chariots copied from the Libyan tribes of the desert. Libyan tribal allies were another important component of the military forces raised by Kyrene. In 308 BC, for example, the Ptolemaic governor of the city was able to raise 10,000 infantrymen and 600 cavalrymen, supplemented by 100 chariots. Of these 10,000 infantrymen, only 8,000 were from Kyrene, the remaining 2,000 being Greek mercenaries (mostly Athenians). After the reign of the early Ptolemies, the use of war chariots was gradually abandoned.

Panoply of a *Psilos*. (*Photo and copyright by Hetairoi*)

Chapter 8

The Seleucid Army

The army of the Seleucid Empire was with without doubt the largest and the strongest of all the Hellenistic armies. It initially inherited most of Alexander the Great's veterans and thus soon became the direct heir of most of the Macedonian military traditions (much more so than the Antigonid Army). The immense dimensions of the Seleucid Empire, which comprised all Macedonian Asia excep Anatolia, obliged the Seleucid military forces to fight against simultaneous menaces on several occasions. The Seleucid Empire was quite an 'artificial' creature from a political point of view, which had important consequences for the destiny of its military forces. As with the Ptolemaic Army, the core of the Seleucid military was represented by the communities of Macedonian military settlers (*kleruchs*): these, unlike in Egypt, were very numerous. Alexander the Great had founded many cities in Asia bearing his name and had encouraged his veteran soldiers to settle in them. The first Seleucid monarchs, especially Seleucus, did everything possible to further develop this system and created even more communities of Macedonian soldiers/farmers. The Macedonian military colonies of the Seleucid Empire were concentrated in the regions of Lydia, Phrygia, northern Syria (the most important and richest region of the empire, where the capital Antioch was located), Mesopotamia and Media. Like with the Ptolemies, the Macedonian military settlers provided much of the manpower for both the 'regular' army (the Royal Guard) and the reserve' army (comprising phalangists and heavy cavalry). The Macedonian military colonists of the Seleucid Empire had the same conditions of service as their Ptolemaic equivalents, but were commonly known as *katoikoi* instead of *kleruchs*; in this chapter we will use the Seleucid version of the term. As with the Ptolemaic Army, the 'regular' and 'reserve' forces were supplemented by large numbers of mercenaries and auxiliaries. The Seleucid Army had the largest number of cavalry and light infantry of the various Hellenistic armies, mostly a result of the Persian influence, since the Seleucid Army was also the direct heir of the Achaemenid military forces (which were based on cavalry and light troops). Native Asian cavalry, in particular, was one of the best branches of the Seleucid Army.

The Royal Guard comprised two different elite regiments of heavy cavalry: that of the Companions and that of the Agema. Each regiment had 1,000 soldiers, organized into five squadrons (*ilai*) of 200 men. The Companions regiment was formed with ex-members of Alexander the Great's 'horse companions', who had settled in the Seleucid

Panoply of a *Thureophoros*. (*Photo and copyright by Hetairoi*)

Empire as *katoikoi*, the Agema regiment from Medes (a race renowned for its skillful horsemanship) from the heart of the empire. Despite being native Asians, the Medes were extremely loyal to the Seleucid royal house. Due to their fidelity, members of the Agema regiment received grants of land exactly as the Macedonian colonists of the Companions regiment. Apparently, after the first generation of settlers disappeared, the Companions regiment started to comprise the youngest and most valorous of the *katoikoi*. These served in the unit during their fathers' lifetimes and then inherited the family farm when they came of age; at this point they became part-time phalangists/ settlers like their fathers, and their young sons replaced them in the Companions regiment. Both regiments escorted the king in battle and were usually assembled together in order to form a powerful heavy cavalry brigade under the direct command of the monarch. The cavalry of the Royal Guard also included a third regiment of light horsemen, initially formed with the Thessalians who had followed Alexander the

Great, who later settled in the town of Larissa (in trans-Jordan) and became military colonists. This unit was commonly known as the *Epilektoi* regiment and numbered 1,000 men like the two heavy cavalry corps. When the region of Media was finally lost to the Parthians around 160 BC, the Agema regiment was disbanded and replaced by the Epilektoi regiment (which was transformed into a heavy cavalry unit). This new corps continued to be known as the Agema regiment and retained the original establishment of 1,000 men. All the cavalrymen of the Seleucid Royal Guard were mounted on magnificent Nisean horses, perfectly suited for heavy cavalrymen. These animals were bred in a royal herd located in Media, which was extremely precious for the Seleucid monarchs.

   The infantry of the Royal Guard was formed by a large and elite division of 10,000 heavy phalangistsknown as the *Argyraspides* ('silver shields'). As is clear from the unit's name, members of this corps were the direct heirs of Alexander the Great's 'Regiment of the Royal Hypaspists', which assumed the denomination of *Argyraspides* during the Indian campaign of 326 BC. Interestingly, however, the Seleucid *Argyraspides* had the same numerical establishment as the Persian Immortals (the Royal Guard of the Achaemenids): this had a clear symbolic meaning. In this case, the Seleucid military structure resulted from a mix of Macedonian and Persian traditions. As we have seen, the original *Argyraspides* had been practically eliminated by Antigonus Monophtalmus; however, according to some scholars, a small number of these old veterans were able to survive the terrible period of service in Arachosia and were later used by Seleucus as the cadre for the new *Argyraspides* division. This elite division was structured on ten large battalions (*lochoi*), each of 1,000 soldiers. The first of these battalions, as in Alexander's Regiment of the Royal Hypaspists, was known as the Vanguard Battalion and performed a series of special duties. Being the foot bodyguard of the monarch, this chosen *lochos* guarded the king's tent on the field and always took the place of honour in the battle-line. In addition, it was frequently used for special missions that required great courage. Members of the *Argyraspides* were chosen from the mass of the *katoikoi* settlers with a precise criterion: every family of colonists having a grant of land had to send one of its young members, who would perform several years of service in the ranks of the *Argyraspides*. Thanks to this system, each young recruit would have developed a strong personal link with the king and received an excellent military training. After service in the *Argyraspides*, these elite phalangists became part-time soldiers of the 'reserve' army, who were reactivated only in time of need. After the Battle of Magnesia in 190 BC, during which the Seleucid phalanxes were defeated by the Roman legions, Antiochus IV decided to reform part of his Royal Guard infantry so as to be able to face the Romans on almost equal terms. As a result, half of the *Argyraspides* were re-equipped as *thorakitai*/'imitation' legionaries with chainmail

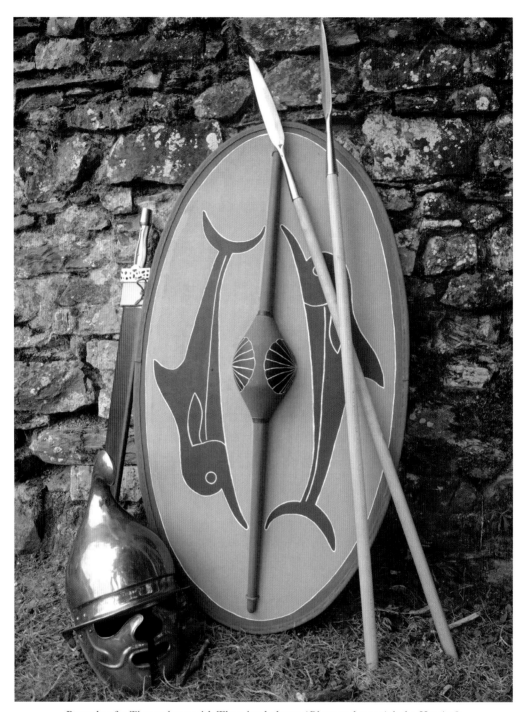

Panoply of a *Thureophoros* with Thracian helmet. (*Photo and copyright by Hetairoi*)

armour; the remaining 5,000 continued to be equipped and trained as traditional phalangists. Since the normal establishment of a Roman legion was 5,000 men, we could say that the *Argyraspides* were effectively divided into an 'imitation' legion of 5,000 soldiers and a standard phalanx of 5,000 heavy infantrymen.

The *katoikoi* of the 'reserve' army were usually mobilized only in wartime and thus lived as normal farmers for most of their lives. Sometimes, however, if the Seleucid monarchs were temporarily out of men, the military colonists could also be used as garrison forces in time of peace. In general, the quality of the Seleucid 'reserve' phalangists was very high, since most of them spent a period of their life (when quite young) serving in the elite *Argyraspides*. The intensive training received during this early period transformed them into skilled soldiers and increased their personal loyalty towards the king. The 'reserve' phalangists, similarly to what happened in Antigonid Macedonia, were organized into two large divisions according to their age: the first division was that of the *Chalkaspides* ('bronze shields'), the second being the *Chryaspides* ('golden shields'). Each division numbered 10,000 men and was structured like the *Argyraspides* division, with ten large *lochoi* of 1,000 soldiers each. The *Chalkaspides* were a sort of active reserve, which could also be employed – if needed –outside the Seleucid borders, while the *Chryaspides* were a more static reserve to be used only inside the empire to face military emergencies, such as a foreign invasion. Members of the *Chalkaspides* were mostly aged between 35 and 45, since younger recruits served in the elite *Argyraspides*; the *Chryaspides* were all skilled veterans and made up a 'national reserve' of experienced soldiers who had already served in the *Chalkaspides* and had passed the age of 45. Together, the three infantry divisions of the Seleucids could deploy 30,000 men; an impressive number compared with the 15,000 Antigonid or 25,000 Ptolemaic phalangists. It is interesting to note that some of the Seleucid military colonies were given to Thracian settlers, who contributed with light infantry contingents to the 'reserve' army, 1,000 Thracian skirmishers being at Raphia in 217 BC.

The *katoikoi* also provided a large part of the Seleucid heavy cavalry, continuing the glorious tradition of the Macedonian 'horse companions' in Asia. Most of the cavalry *katoikoi* were settled in Syria (the heart of the Seleucid Empire) or Media (where the best Nisean horses could be found). Apparently, these military settlers provided 6,000 heavy cavalrymen. Like the cavalry of the Royal Guard, these were organized into regiments of 1,000 men each. All six regiments were in turn divided into five squadrons (*ilai*) of 200 men each. Like the two divisions of the 'reserve' infantry, the cavalry *katoikoi* served in 'territorial' units because each regiment was formed with colonists coming from the same settlement. Initially, the *katoikoi* cavalry was equipped more or less as the former Macedonian 'horse companions', but later the Seleucid

Panoply of a *Thorakites*. (*Photo and copyright by Hetairoi*)

heavy cavalry was completely re-equipped and all its members became super-heavy cataphracts. Basically, a cataphract was a cavalryman fighting with full armour and riding an armoured horse (the latter could be partly or fully armoured). This kind of heavy cavalry had been used in the steppes of central Asia for centuries, with great success, and was gradually adopted by the Asiatic cavalry contingents from the eastern satrapies of the Persian Empire and thus came in contact with the Macedonians with the fall of the Achaemenids. During the last campaigns of his life, Alexander the Great had to face Asian cataphracts and apparently was quite impressed by them. Generally speaking, the cataphracts were much heavier than the Macedonian 'horse companions'. When Alexander invaded Asia, however, the contingents of super-heavy cavalry included in the Persian Army were still quite small from a numerical point of view. After the Macedonian conquest, in order to face more effectively the 'horse companions', the Asian rulers of the eastern territories started to encourage the development of cataphract cavalry contingents. In 209-205 BC, the Seleucid king Antiochus III had to fight a series of harsh campaigns against the rebel satraps of the eastern provinces. During these difficult military operations, conducted at the limits of central Asia, the Seleucid monarch had to face large contingents of eastern cataphracts. Antiochus III was very impressed by the military capabilities of the latter and decided to transform his own *katoikoi* cavalry into cataphracts. By 190 BC, when the Seleucids fought against the Romans at Magnesia, all the *katoikoi* cavalrymen had received the new equipment and training as cataphracts. This rapid transformation was possible thanks to the large employment of Nisean horses by the Seleucids: these strong animals were perfect to use the new kind of defensive equipment.

Light troops (both infantry and cavalry) were provided by two different sources: mercenaries and Asian subjects. Generally, however, the Seleucids employed less mercenaries than the Ptolemies. The most common mercenaries were Greek/Anatolian *thureophoroi* and Cretan archers. At Raphia, for example, there were 5,000 mercenary *thureophoroi* and 2,500 Cretans. Apparently, the 2,500 Cretan archers formed a sort of permanent corps during most of Antiochus III's reign. Like the Attalids of Pergamon, the Seleucids signed treaties with several Cretan towns which regulated the recruiting of mercenaries. During the years of Demetrius II's reign, the Cretan mercenaries in Seleucid service became powerful enough to control the political life of the empire: this violent period of the Seleucid history, known as the 'Cretan Terror', ended only when the 'regular' and 'reserve' troops finally defeated and destroyed the Cretans (who had terrorized and looted most of the empire, including Antioch). Tarantine light cavalrymen were also employed, albeit in small numbers. When we speak of 'Tarantine' light cavalry for the Hellenistic armies, we should bear in mind that this term indicates mercenary horsemen from Taras only for the early Hellenistic period; over time, the term 'Tarantine' started to indicate all mercenaries (mostly Greek) equipped like the original light cavalrymen from Taras. The word 'Tarantine' no longer bore a geographical significance, but was used purely as a tactical term. Tarantine horsemen were light skirmishers equipped similarly to the Thessalians of Alexander the Great, with javelins and shield (and no armour). Minor groups of mercenaries included Thracians (either light infantrymen or light cavalrymen) and Galatians. First employed under Seleucus II (247-226 BC) after their settlement in central Anatolia, the Galatians fought in great numbers for Antiochus III at Magnesia (3,000 infantrymen and 2,500 cavalrymen). The peace treaty between the Seleucids and Rome, signed in

Panoply of a 'Horse companion'. (*Photo and copyright by Hetairoi*)

189 BC after the Battle of Magnesia, officially forbade the recruiting of troops west of the Taurus Mountains for the Seleucids. In spite of the treaty, however, the Hellenistic monarchs of Syria continued to use Galatian mercenaries in their army. Antiochus IV, for example, had 5,000 loyal Celtic warriors.

Asian light troops were provided by a variety of different peoples, from every corner of the empire. The status of these auxiliary troops is frequently quite difficult to determine: they could be subjects, allies sent by vassal kings or mercenaries. In general, the only area of the Seleucid Empire that did not provide 'native' levies was Syria: since the latter was the most important region of their state, the Seleucids always preferred to not recruit locals to avoid the outbreak of popular revolts. Similarly to what happened in the Attalid city of Pergamon, the Greek cities of Syria had some sort of citizen militia formed of both infantrymen and cavalrymen. These militias, the most important of which was that of Antioch (the Seleucid capital), were usually employed only as garrison troops in their home cities. In case of military emergencies, however, they could be used to defend their territory from foreign aggression. Both the infantry and cavalry of the urban militias were generally equipped as *thureophoroi*. The light troops of the various Asian peoples consisted of foot skirmishers and horse skirmishers; mounted archers were also quite common, albeit being few in numbers. In general, it was standard Hellenistic practice to raise mercenary contingents of light-armed troops from potentially rebellious tribesmen, with the objective of 'normalizing' the young men who would have been most naturally inclined towards violent and rebellious behaviour. At the Battle of Raphia, the following Asian auxiliaries were present: 10,000 Arabs (including camel troops); 5,000 Dahai, Carmanians and Cilicians; 5,000 Medes, Kissians and Cadusians; 2,000 Persian archers and slingers (mercenaries); 500 Lydians; and 1,000 Kurds. The Arabs were frequently employed by the Seleucids for desert operations, like the Persians before them; during the Hellenistic period, the various Arab tribes generally switched alliances between Seleucid and Ptolemies as the control of Palestine changed. At the Battle of Magnesia, the following Asian auxiliaries were deployed by the Seleucids: 3,000 Trallians; 1,500 Carians and Cilicians; 2,500 Mysians; 2,000 Kappadokians; 8,000 Elymaian archers and Kyrtii slingers; and 4,000 Pisidians, Pamphylians and Lykians. At the Daphnae Parade of 165 BC, the army of Antiochus IV included the following mercenary or Asian contingents: 5,000 Mysian mercenaries (equipped as *thureophoroi*), 3,000 Cilicians (equipped as javelineers), 3,000 Thracian mercenaries and 5,000 Galatian warriors.

The Seleucid Army had the largest number of war elephants among the various Hellenistic military forces. Its elephant corps was also formed by massive Indian pachyderms (much bigger and stronger than any elephant from North Africa). In many respects, the elephant corps was the real 'elite' of the Seleucid Army: no other Hellenistic military force could deploy so many war elephants and with such a high level of training. Seleucus was the initiator of the Seleucid elephant corps, as during the early phase of his reign he concluded a peace treaty with the Indian king Chandragupta Maurya according to which the Indians were to provide 500 pachyderms to the Seleucids. At the Battle of Ipsos, Seleucus deployed 400 war elephants. When Antiochus I fought against the Galatians in 273 BC, the Seleucid elephant corps had

Different models of Hellenistic helmets. (*Photo and copyright by Hetairoi*)

reduced to just twenty beasts, yet sixteen of these proved to be the key factor in the decisive victory of the Seleucids over the Celtic invaders. Antiochus III had just ten elephants at the beginning of his reign, but was later able to increase their number to 100 thanks to massive trade with the Indian kingdoms. For his large expedition against the rebel eastern satraps, he was able to obtain another fifty pachyderms by exacting them from Bactrian and Indian vassal kings. When the Parthians conquered most of the Seleucid eastern provinces around the middle of the second century BC, the Seleucids lost any possibility to buy elephants from India. Finally, according to the Treaty of Apamea that followed the defeat of Magnesia, the Seleucids were obliged by the Romans to cede their elephant corps to the Kingdom of Pergamon. In battle, the war elephants were generally brigaded with contingents of light infantrymen, who could protect their exposed flanks from enemy attacks. On most occasions, each pachyderm was protected by forty to fifty foot skirmishers. After expanding his elephant corps

Boeotian, Pilos, Attic-Boeotian and Apulian helmets (from left to right). (*Photo and copyright by Hetairoi*)

Thracian, Thracian-Phrygian and Phrygian helmets (from left to right). (*Photo and copyright by Hetairoi*)

to 150 beasts, Antiochus III organized the 'guard' soldiers of each elephant into fixed units of fifty men, so each war elephant became a real 'tactical unit' comprising some escort troops.

It is interesting to note that the Seleucids were the only Hellenistic monarchs to employ scythed chariots in their armies. Clearly this peculiarity was inherited from the military traditions of the Persians, who employed large numbers of war chariots against Alexander the Great at the Battle of Gaugamela. Seleucus deployed more than 100 scythed chariots at the Battle of Ipsos, while Antiochus III had just a few of them at Magnesia against the Romans. The presence of war chariots gradually disappeared from the Seleucid Army over time. They were probably eliminated from the Seleucid military forces as a result of the heavy cavalry conversion into cataphracts: the tactical functions of the chariots and the new super-heavy cavalry were more or less the same. According to contemporary sources, the personal equipment of the charioteers was also very similar to that of the cataphracts.

Attic helmets (left) and Macedonian–Attic helmet (right). (*Photo and copyright by Hetairoi*)

Sidon, Boeotian, Attic-Boeotian and Attic helmets (from left to right). (*Photo and copyright by Hetairoi*)

Chapter 9

The Attalid Army

As we have seen, the Kingdom of Pergamon originated from Lysimachus' possessions in western and central Anatolia. After the death of the old master of Thrace, one of his officers (named Philetaerus) took control of the important city of Pergamon and started a new Hellenistic dynasty. Initially, Philetaerus never formally claimed independence for his new kingdom, but proclaimed himself as a vassal of the Seleucids. Over time, however, it soon became clear that the Kingdom of Pergamon was a fully autonomous state, and Eumenes I, the successor of Philetaerus, was the first monarch of Pergamon to proclaim the independence of his kingdom. In the following decades the Attalids fought several wars against the Seleucids, especially for possession of southern Anatolia. Despite being much smaller than their enemies, they were able to win on several occasions. Once Rome became part of the Hellenistic political world, the Kingdom of Pergamon became the most loyal and important local ally of the newcomers. When the Roman-Seleucid War broke out in 192 BC, the Attalids obviously sided with Rome against their old enemies. Thanks to this intelligent choice, they were able to obtain some important territorial gains at the end of the war, including the strategic Seleucid lands located west of the Taurus Mountains. In 133 BC, the last Attalid king, Attalus III, died without an heir. In order to prevent the outbreak of a civil war that would have destroyed his flourishing realm, he bequeathed the whole of Pergamon to the Roman Republic. As a result, Rome obtained most of Anatolia without fighting and could form the new province of Asia.

Pergamon was never a major military power of the Hellenistic world, mainly because there were no military settlements of Macedonian/Greek colonists in the territory of western and central Anatolia. As a result of this, the Attalids could never form phalanxes with native Macedonians and were thus obliged to rely on mercenaries or Asian troops. In addition, the general Graeco-Macedonian population of the kingdom was very small compared with that of the other Hellenistic states, with the notable exception of the city of Pergamon, which had a citizen militia formed by local inhabitants of Graeco-Macedonian descent. This militia, however, was only employed for garrison duties and not to fight in pitched battles. In general, the Attalid armies were formed of three categories of troops: Anatolian light cavalry, traditional peltasts (mercenary Greeks or Anatolians) and light infantrymen (mercenary Cretan archers or Asian skirmishers).

Detail of a Phrygian helmet. (*Photo and copyright by Hetairoi*)

At the Battle of Magnesia in 190 BC, the decisive clash of the Roman–Seleucid War, the Attalid Army deployed the following troops: 800 Anatolian cavalrymen, 3,000 peltasts, 500 Cretan archers and 500 skirmishers of the Trallian tribe (a Thracian people settled in Anatolia). It is important to note that the portion of Anatolia controlled by Pergamon was inhabited for centuries by several tribes of Thracian descent, the most important from a military point of view being the Phrygians. Cretan mercenary archers were a very important component of the Attalid Army: their employment was officially regulated from 183 BC by a treaty signed between Pergamon and several Cretan towns. The most important Anatolian subjects of the Attalids were the Mysians, who served both as javelineers and *thureophoroi*. After the occupation of the Seleucid territories located west of the Taurus Mountains, a number of Mysians were sent to the newly conquered territories as military settlers. With the foundation of these new military colonies after 189 BC, which were based on the model of the Macedonian *kleruchs*, it seems that the Attalids started to reduce the number of mercenaries in their military forces. Despite fighting against them on several occasions, the monarchs of Pergamon frequently employed Galatians as mercenaries. Once these Celts settled in central Anatolia, the Attalids made use of their excellent light cavalry contingents. It is also interesting to note that the Kingdom of Pergamon acquired the elephant corps of the Seleucids after the latter's defeat at Magnesia. After the death of these war elephants – the survivors of the fifty-four deployed by the Seleucids against Rome – the Attalids had no access to more pachyderms.

Detail of an Attic-Boeotian helmet. (*Photo and copyright by Hetairoi*)

Chapter 10

Hellenistic Anatolia

During the Hellenistic period, Hellenistic Anatolia contained three small political entities that co-existed with the Kingdom of Pergamon: the Kingdom of Bithynia, the Kingdom of Cappadocia and Galatia. The Bithynians were one of the Thracian tribes that had migrated from Europe (modern Bulgaria) to Anatolia, just like the more numerous Phrygians. Despite being formally subjects of the Persian Empire, since 435 BC (well before the arrival of Alexander the Great) they had started to act as an independent realm. From 297 BC the rulers of Bithynia started to call themselves kings, becoming fully autonomous in 281 after the death of Lysimachus. Nicomedes I, ascending to the Bithynian throne in 280, was the first monarch to launch a significant process of 'hellenization' in his realm: until then, the Bithynians had continued to fight as light infantrymen (traditional peltasts) like every Thracian tribe. Under Nicomedes I, the Bithynian warriors started to be re-equipped as *thureophoroi* and progressively abandoned their Thracian military traditions. We have no idea of their numbers, but they were surely supplemented by contingents of Galatian and Thracian mercenaries on several occasions. Apparently, some of the later Bithynian kings had a personal bodyguard formed by 500 Thracian mercenaries from Europe. Bithynian mounted troops included both light horsemen (a sort of mounted *thureophoroi*) and heavy cavalrymen (the nobility of the country). Generally speaking, being unable to rely on a professional body of phalangists or large corps of mercenaries, the Bithynians had to count on a small army formed by native citizens. It must also be remembered that the Bithynians were frequently employed as mercenaries by other Hellenistic states, especially by the Ptolemies of Egypt. In 74 BC, the last monarch of Bithynia, having no heirs, bequeathed his kingdom to Rome like the last Attalid ruler of Pergamon.

The independent Kingdom of Cappadocia was founded in 331 BC by Ariarathes, the last Persian governor of the Cappadocian satrapy. Since the Macedonians continued their advance towards the heart of the Persian Empire without attacking Cappadocia, Ariarathes was able to retain power in his own province and avoided a direct confrontation with the army of Alexander the Great. Ariarathes was defeated and killed by Perdiccas in 322 BC, but after a brief period of Macedonian occupation, Cappadocia became again independent in 301 under Ariarathes' son. The latter initiated a new royal family

Detail of an Apulian helmet. (*Photo and copyright by Hetairoi*)

that was to last until 96 BC, when Mithridates VI of Pontus invaded Cappadocia and briefly annexed it to his possessions. With the defeat of Pontus, however, the Romans decided to install a new royal family in Cappadocia and transformed the small realm into a client kingdom. In 36 BC, the last exponent of this new dynasty died without heirs and thus the Romans gave Cappadocia to a local noble named Archelaus, who was a personal friend of Mark Antony. When also Archelaus died in 17 AD, Cappadocia was absorbed into the Roman Empire. The Kingdom of Cappadocia initially remained strongly linked to the military traditions of the Persian Empire, but from 255 BC the Cappadocian monarchs started a general process of 'hellenization' that also affected the army. The information we have on Cappadocian armed forces is very scarce. What we know for sure is that Ariarathes commanded an army of 30,000 infantry and 15,000 cavalry against Perdiccas. After his death, the Cappadocians became a fundamental part of Eumenes' army. Being formally vassals of the Seleucids for several decades, the Cappadocians sent auxiliary contingents to support their masters on various occasions. At Magnesia, for example, there were 2,000 Cappadocians equipped as *thureophoroi*. Apparently, with the 'hellenization' of their army the Cappadocians abandoned the traditional Persian light equipment and transformed themselves into *thureophoroi*.

When the Celts invaded the southern Balkans in 280 BC, their hordes included 152,000 foot warriors and 61,000 horsemen. A number of these later crossed the Hellespont and went to Anatolia. Apparently the Celtic invaders came to Asia at the invitation of Nicomedes I, King of Bithynia, who wanted their military help in a dynastic struggle against his brother. The Galatians settling in the centre of Anatolia belonged to three different tribes: the Tectosages, Trocmi and Tolistobogii. These settled on the plateau of Phrygia, after subduing the local inhabitants of Thracian descent. This region, where the modern city of Ankara is located, soon started to be known as Galatia. The three tribes organized themselves into a loose federation, which exerted control over the subject Phrygian peasants. The Galatians in Anatolia could originally field a total of 10,000 warriors, which was later increased after the settlement became permanent. The Celts arrived in Anatolia with 160 war chariots of the conventional two-horse type used in Celtic Europe. After settling in their new mountainous territory, however, the Galatians gradually abandoned the practice of using war chariots in battle. During the early phase of their settlement, the Galatians mostly supported themselves by plundering bordering countries or by serving as mercenaries in the various Hellenistic armies of the time. In 232 BC, the Attalids of Pergamon finally defeated them in battle, which eventually led to the creation of a more permanent Galatian settlement in central Anatolia that became a vassal of Pergamon. In 189 BC, after defeating the Seleucids at Magnesia, the Romans launched a large expedition against the Celts of Anatolia that became known as the Galatian War. After being defeated, the Galatians lost much of

Detail of a 'kausia' cap. (*Photo and copyright by Hetairoi*)

their military power and were later invaded by Mithridates VI of Pontus. Thanks to the decisive help of the Romans, however, the Celts of Anatolia were later able to regain their independence after the end of the Mithridatic Wars (88-63 BC) between Pontus and the Roman Republic. In 62 BC, Galatia formally became a client state of Rome and was officially organized as a kingdom; in 25 BC, this Kingdom of Galatia was finally annexed by the Romans.

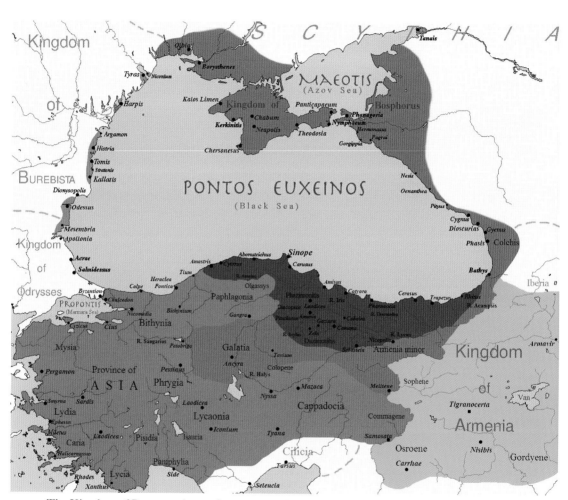

The Kingdom of Pontus at the maximum extent. (*Public domain pictures from Wikimedia Commons*)

Chapter 11

Pontus, Armenia and the Bosporan Kingdom

T he Kingdom of Pontus was founded in 281 BC by Mithridates I, who initiated a new Persian dynasty in the north-east of Anatolia by creating a new state. The region of Pontus, located south of the Black Sea on the northern coast of Anatolia, was part of Cappadocia under the Persian Empire and was later conquered by Alexander the Great. The Mithridatic royal house, which ruled Pontus from 281, belonged to the highest level of the Persian nobility: before Alexander the Great, members of this family had been the satraps of Phrygia. The arrival of the Macedonians, however, did not change their situation because they recognized Alexander as the new emperor and thus were able to retain their possessions. In 302 BC Antigonus Monophtalmus had invaded Phrygia and killed the ruling Mithridatic satrap, whose son, despite the difficult situation, was able to escape with just a few loyal retainers. After abandoning Phrygia, he reached the north-east of Anatolia, where he founded a new independent kingdom by assembling together the areas of northern Cappadocia and eastern Paphlagonia. From 281, this new king assumed the name of Mithridates I and proclaimed the royal dignity of his family. During the following decades, the various monarchs of Pontus fought against the other Anatolian states and the Galatians in order to expand their dominions. The military forces of Pontus also launched a series of military campaigns against Greek cities located on the northern coast of Anatolia. The Mithridatic kings had no access to the Mediterranean and thus had to find an alternative for trade and commerce: this alternative was represented by the Black Sea, which soon became the centre of all Pontic economic and political activities. After conquering the Greek cities of the coast, Pontic expansionism invested the southern part of modern Ukraine (the region of Crimea) and the western coast of the Caucasus. The Pontic kings gradually created a very strong political and economic relation with the Greek cities (colonies) on the northern coast of the Black Sea, and similar links were made with the Greek colonies of the Thracian coast (in the eastern part of modern Bulgaria). As a result of all these moves, the Pontic rulers gradually became the real masters of the Black Sea. Initially, the Romans did not consider them as a serious menace, partly because Rome had no interests in the northern part of the Black Sea. This situation changed in 116 BC with the ascendancy to the Pontic throne of Mithridates VI, who had great political ambitions over the whole of Anatolia. Since

150 BC the Kingdom of Pontus had been gradually 'hellenized' by the Mithridatic monarchs, who partly abandoned their Persian traditions in favour of a modernization of their country. The results of this process were clearly visible during the reign of Mithridates VI.

Unlike previous kings of Pontus, including his father, Mithridates VI followed a strong anti-Roman agenda from the beginning of his reign. The main political ambition of the new king was to unite the whole Hellenistic world against Rome in order to restore the multinational empire of Alexander the Great. Differently from other Hellenistic monarchs, Mithridates perfectly understood the spirit of Alexander the Great's political vision: he wanted to create a new multinational state in which

The Kingdom of Armenia at the maximum extent. (*CC BY-SA 3.0, Wikimedia User 'Nareklm'*)

peoples with different traditions and cultures could live and prosper in peace. The usual divisions between Macedonians/Greeks and Asian subjects had no sense for the new Pontic king, who was not of Macedonian descent. During the early phase of his reign, Mithridates conquered a large portion of Armenia (south of the Caucasus region) and the strategic Kingdom of Colchis (on the western coast of the Caucasus). The latter, in particular, was rich in natural resources: gold, wax, hemp and honey. In 101 BC, after having secured his 'empire' in the Black Sea region, Mithridates started to expand in Anatolia and invaded the Kingdom of Cappadocia, which was given to his infant son. During the following years, the ambitious Pontic king also formed a strong alliance with the Kingdom of Armenia, which was now ruled by Tigranes II, who had married Mithridates' daughter, Cleopatra. These events made it clear to the Roman Republic that the expansionism of Pontus had to be stopped as soon as possible.

The First Mithridatic War broke out in 90 BC, the military forces of Pontus invading the Kingdom of Bithynia and then marching across the Roman province of Asia (the former Kingdom of Pergamon). Local Roman forces were unable to resist and thus abandoned most of Anatolia in the hands of Mithridates. The Pontic invasion was supported by the public opinion of the Anatolians, who hated the Romans and their system of heavy taxation. In 88 BC, to present himself as the 'restorer' of Hellenistic freedom, Mithridates ordered the execution of 80,000 Romans and Italics living in the province of Asia. In the following months, most of the Greek cities, formally allied with Rome, joined Pontus in the war of 'liberation' against the foreign invaders. Athens, in particular, had a prominent role in this process. In 87 BC, the Romans, under Sulla, besieged the city with a massive army. Despite the military support of Pontus, Athens was finally occupied by Sulla. During the following years, the Romans defeated the Pontic Army in Greece on two occasions; as a result, Mithridates was forced to abandon Greece and come to terms with Rome. According to the peace treaty of 85 BC, Pontus had to relinquish all the territories that had been occupied in Anatolia: the Kingdom of Cappadocia, the Kingdom of Bithynia and the Roman province of Asia. But the military capabilities of Mithridates in Asia were still intact. The Second Mithridatic War was fought from 83-81 BC, but remained a local conflict that was fought on a small scale between the Roman military forces of Asia and part of Mithridates' army. At the end of the skirmishes that made up this conflict, nothing had changed from a territorial point of view. In the following years, the ambitious Pontic monarch started to form new alliances against the Romans. He allied with the pirates of Cilicia (who had not yet been completely defeated by the Romans) and with the Roman usurper Quintus Sertorius (who ruled the Roman territories of Spain, which had temporarily seceded from the central government of the Republic). The contribution of these new allies was vitally important for Pontus. In 75 BC, the last monarch of Bithynia died

Detail of a 'kausia' cap. (*Photo and copyright by Hetairoi*)

without heirs and left his kingdom to Rome, but two years later Mithridates invaded Bithynia and caused the outbreak of the Third Mithridatic War.

This time, however, military operations were quite favourable to the Romans from the beginning. The Pontic Army had to retreat inside the borders of Pontus, while Mithridates tried in every possible way to avoid a direct military confrontation with the Roman legions. In order to achieve his objective, the Pontic king fled to Armenia, where he could count on the support of his ally, Tigranes II. During the summer of 69 BC, the Romans invaded Armenia and defeated Tigranes II in a vast pitched battle, fought outside the Armenian capital of Tigranocerta. While the Romans were fighting against the remaining forces of Tigranes II in northern Armenia, Mithridates again invaded Pontus in order to reconquer his kingdom. This time the Pontic king was able to defeat the Romans in battle, leading to a great change in the strategic situation of the war. The Roman military forces now risked being isolated from their lines of supply, so had to abandon Armenia and could not defeat decisively Tigranes II. The following months were very difficult for Rome, as Mithridates completed the reconquest of Pontus and the Armenians invaded Cappadocia. In 66 BC, however, Pontus and Armenia had to face the enormous military power of Pompey the Great (who had recently crushed the Cilician pirates in the south of Anatolia). Pompey concluded a military alliance with the Parthians, who attacked Armenia and kept Tigranes II busy in the east. At the same time he marched with all his forces against Pontus. This time Mithridates was finally defeated in a large pitched battle and obliged to flee, the defeated king marching with his few surviving forces to Colchis and then to Crimea. Meanwhile, in 65 BC, Pompey invaded Armenia and defeated Tigranes II. Mithridates was killed during the following months, while reorganizing his military forces for a defence of Crimea. Apparently his death was caused by a revolt of the army, led by his son, Pharnaces. As a result of the war, the western half of Pontus was annexed by Rome; the eastern part was transformed into a small client kingdom that continued to exist until AD 62. The Crimean possessions of Pontus, under the guidance of Pharnaces, became the new Bosporan Kingdom (a vassal state of Rome, which carried on until AD 340).

The early Pontic Army retained all the military traditions dating back to the Persian period, and thus was largely composed of light troops (both foot and mounted). The original territorial nucleus of Pontus was located in a peripheral zone of the Hellenistic world and so had no Macedonian/Greek military settlements inside its borders. Around 150 BC, however, the Pontic monarchs started to transform their army into a Hellenistic military force, which was achieved by mixing Macedonian organization/tactics for infantry with Persian organization/tactics for cavalry. In general terms, the army of Mithridates VI was always a very multinational force: the ambitious king tried to develop a unified cultural identity among the different peoples living around the

Detail of a 'petasos' cap made of straw. (*Photo and copyright by Hetairoi*)

Black Sea region, in order to unite them against Rome and bind them to his personal power. In addition to his subjects, Mithridates could count on several different sources of mercenaries/allies: Greeks, Thracians, Galatians, Scythians and Sarmatians. All these peoples lived around the Black Sea and could provide Pontus with different kinds of troop types; Scythians and Sarmatians, in particular, were famous for their contingents of cataphracts and mounted archers. Funds to pay mercenaries were not a problem, while the local levies of Pontic peasants provided strong and resilient recruits who were accustomed to live and fight in mountainous terrain.

From 150 BC, the local Pontic infantrymen started to be equipped and trained as phalangists and abandoned their previous style of fighting based on old Persian models. Under Mithridates VI, the new 'hellenized' contingents of the Pontic Army were reorganized. It is important to remember, however, that the largest part of Mithridates' military forces continued to be composed of Asian light infantrymen or cavalrymen. The core of the Pontic infantry was represented by the phalanx, which was organized as an independent division of 15,000 men. Its members were known as *Chalkaspides* ('bronze shields') and were equipped as heavy infantrymen. However, the quality of Mithridates' phalanx was not comparable to that of other Hellenistic armies: Pontic phalangists were peasant levies and not professionals. In addition, in order to increase the number of his *Chalkaspides* in view of the war against Rome, it seems that Mithridates also recruited substantial numbers of freed slaves. After defeat in the First Mithridatic War, Mithridates decided to reform his heavy infantry by abandoning the traditional organization based on the phalanx. It is interesting to note that the peace treaty signed with Sulla obliged him to expel all the freed slaves from his armies, so he had to rely on alternative sources of manpower. The total number of the heavy infantrymen was increased from 15,000 to 36,000, organized into sixty *cohortes* of 600 soldiers each, following the internal organization of the Roman legions (which were structured on *cohortes*). Of these sixty new units, ten were made up of *thorakitai* (imitation legionaries) and fifty of *thureophoroi* (medium infantrymen). Apparently the 6,000 Pontic 'legionaries' were equipped and trained under the guidance of two exiled Roman officers, probably sent by Quintus Sertorius (who fought against Pompey in Rome's civil wars), far from Roman eyes, in Crimea and Armenia. Despite all these efforts, the Pontic imitation legionaries proved to be no match for the real Roman legionaries.

The heavy cavalry of Mithridates included an elite squadron of 'horse companions', formed by the nobility of Pontus and all the personal retainers of the king, who came from every corner of Anatolia. We have no precise details about this unit, but know that its members were equipped as cataphracts. Presumably the squadron had 400 soldiers like most of the Hellenistic *agema* squadrons. The rest of the Pontic heavy cavalry were mercenary/allied cataphracts provided by different peoples: Cappadocians, Armenians, Scythians and Sarmatians. As in Armenia, cataphracts had been introduced into Pontus during the Persian age. It seems, however, that the best cataphracts under the orders of Mithridates were the Cappadocian ones. Apparently heavy cavalry was the real elite of Mithridates' army and the component that caused most trouble to the Romans. The Pontic cataphracts were usually supplemented by large numbers of scythed chariots, in perfect Persian fashion, but these proved to be of no use against the Roman legions and were progressively abandoned after the end of the First Mithridatic War.

Light infantry and light cavalry were both provided by the multinational contingents of allies/mercenaries, which were very numerous but sometimes of little military value. The Greeks came from the colonies of northern Anatolia, Caucasus and Crimea; apparently, they mostly served as heavy infantrymen. The Thracians were not very numerous and fought in their usual manner as light skirmishers, while the Galatians were employed as heavy infantrymen with large oval shields. Scythians mostly provided excellent contingents of horse archers, while Sarmatians could be employed either as cataphracts or as mounted archers. Another source of light troops was the Cilician and Cretan pirates, who were allies of Pontus against Rome. Thanks to his large economic resources, Mithridates was even able to pay for the services of entire Cilician or Cretan mercenary fleets, since Pontus had no navy. Generally speaking, Pontic armies were quite large. In 86 BC, for example, Mithridates deployed the following forces against

Linothorax, scale armour, leather muscle cuirass and bronze muscle cuirass (from left to right). (*Photo and copyright by Hetairoi*)

the Romans: 20,000 Pontic, Cappadocian, Scythian and Sarmatian cavalry; 100,000 infantrymen (15,000 of whom were *Chalkaspides*, the rest being light troops); and sixty scythed chariots.

The history of the Kingdom of Armenia was very similar to that of Pontus. Until the arrival of Alexander the Great, Armenia was a satrapy of the Persian Empire. After Alexander's death, the Orontids (the dynasty of satraps that ruled Armenia under the Persians) proclaimed themselves kings and made Armenia an independent state in 321 BC. Until 95 BC, Armenia remained a minor Hellenistic power, playing little part in the wars of that period. The ascendancy of Tigranes II, however, changed all this. One of Tigranes' first political acts was to form a solid alliance with Mithridates of Pontus: one of his objectives was creating a solid military coalition that could face on almost equal terms both the Romans and the Parthians. Tigranes' first military campaigns were conducted against the Parthians. These were particularly successful and led to the Armenian occupation of some important Mesopotamian territories. In 82 BC, Syrian nobles who wished to cancel the last vestiges of the Seleucid Empire offered the throne of their country to Tigranes. The Armenian monarch accepted the offer and transformed himself, albeit only for a brief period, into the master of Hellenistic Asia. During this period he even built a magnificent new capital bearing his name, Tigranocerta. Defeated in battle together with Mithridates, Tigranes had to face the subsequent invasion of Armenia launched by Pompey. Defeated again by

Example of linothorax. (*Photo and copyright by Hetairoi*)

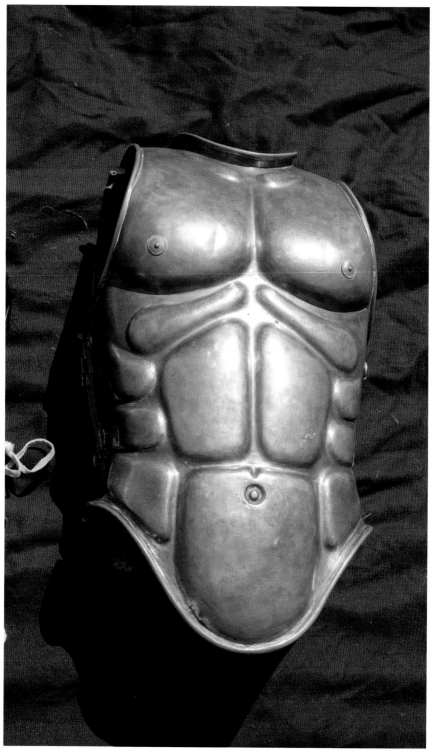

Example of bronze muscle cuirass. (*Photo and copyright by Hetairoi*)

the Romans and attacked also by the Parthians, Tigranes was obliged to come to terms with his enemies. After these events Armenia lost the major part of its new territories (including Syria) and was transformed into a client state of Rome. The Kingdom of Armenia continued to exist as a buffer state between the Romans and the Parthians until AD 428, acting as a battlefield between the two powers. The Armenian Army was not very 'hellenized', remaining strongly influenced by Persian military traditions. Basically, the Armenian Army was a heavy cavalry force of cataphracts supported by auxiliary contingents of light cavalry and light infantry. Light cavalry consisted of mounted archers, while light infantry were mostly javelineers, but also included contingents of archers and slingers. During the reign of Tigranes II, however, the Armenians could also deploy large contingents of allies/vassals from newly conquered regions. In 69 BC, the Armenian Army deployed the following troops: 16,000 cataphracts, 18,000 mounted archers, 20,000 allied/vassal light cavalrymen (equipped as mounted skirmishers), 150,000 infantrymen (with light equipment, including allies/vassals) and 20,000 missile troops (archers and slingers). Apparently, 6,000 of the cataphracts acted as a mounted bodyguard for the king, being known as *Ayrudzi*. These elite soldiers were a 'regular' central army, formed by professionals.

The Greeks, starting from the seventh century BC, had begun to found several colonies on the Crimean coast of the Black Sea. These small centres, initially created just to act as commercial outposts, soon transformed themselves into large and rich cities that controlled the trade routes of the northern Black Sea. The Greek colonies of Crimea became fundamental in the development of strong commercial relations between the nomadic peoples of the Ukrainian steppes (Scythians and Sarmatians) and the Greek world. Thanks to the massive exporting of wheat and grain, the Greek colonies of Crimea soon started to flourish and became increasingly important from a political point of view. Around 480 BC, probably to have better military defence against the menace represented by the local peoples of the steppes, the various Greek colonies of Crimea decided to unite themselves and formed a kingdom that was a 'confederation' of cities. In 438 BC, the legitimate royal house of this kingdom was removed by a usurper named Spartocus, who soon initiated his own dynasty. The Spartocid royal house was able to expand its dominions by conquering new territories in southern Ukraine and submitting several Scythian tribes. In 310 BC, the expansionism of the Spartocids was temporarily stopped by the outbreak of a civil war, which also caused some trouble to the flourishing economy of the kingdom. Around 108 BC, Paerisades V, the last king of the Spartocids, was obliged to ask for Pontic military help against the increasing pressure of the steppe peoples. As a result, after the death of Paerisades, Greek Crimea was absorbed into the multinational empire of Mithridates. After the death of the great Pontic monarch, the Greek kingdom of Crimea again became an independent state and started to be known as the Bosporan Kingdom. This remained a vassal of Rome

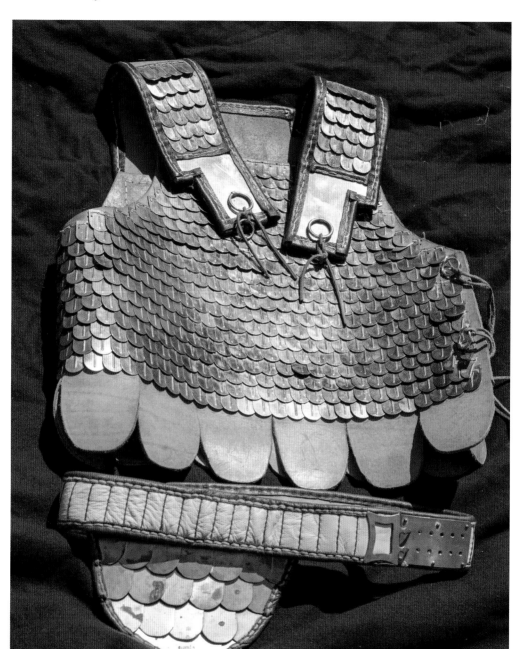

Example of scale armour. (*Photo and copyright by Hetairoi*)

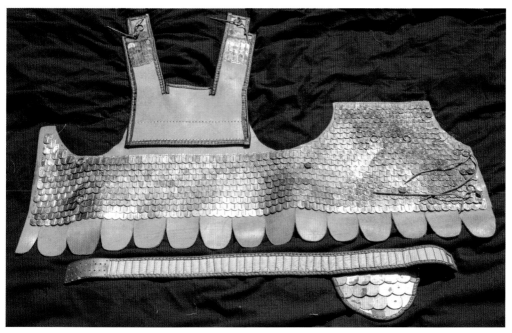

Detail of a scale cuirass. (*Photo and copyright by Hetairoi*)

during the following three centuries, receiving frequent Roman military assistance against the steppe peoples, mostly in the form of military garrisons. Around 340 BC, the Bosporan Kingdom was finally destroyed by the Huns, who were moving from central Asia into Europe.

The military organization of the Greek colonies founded in Crimea was initially exactly the same as the cities located in mainland Greece: each colony had its own small army of citizens/soldiers, who fought as hoplites. As the Greek colonies became increasingly rich, the use of citizens/soldiers started to decrease considerably. Thanks to the vast amounts of money obtained from trade, the Greek colonists were able to raise substantial contingents of mercenaries. By 310 BC, the majority of soldiers serving in the military forces of the Greek colonies in Crimea were mercenaries. During the civil war of that year, the two opposing sides deployed the following troops: 2,000 Greek mercenaries, 2,000 Thracian mercenaries, 20,000 allied Scythian infantry and 10,000 allied Scythian cavalry on one side; and 22,000 allied Scythian infantry and 20,000 allied Scythian cavalry on the other. As is clear from these numbers, Scythians were readily available for service as allies/subjects and could provide extremely large contingents. Ukraine was the home of the Scythians, who were famous in the ancient world for their great capabilities as horse archers. In addition to light cavalrymen, they could deploy also large bodies of heavy cavalry (with full armour, also for horses). All the Scythian infantrymen were equipped as light skirmishers. In general, most of the

Example of leather muscle cuirass. (*Photo and copyright by Hetairoi*)

Scythian tribes fought in the armies of the Crimean Greeks as allies; some of them, however, had been subdued by the Greeks and thus sent their men as subjects. Sources of mercenaries also included Galatians and Paphlagonians from Anatolia, who were sometimes employed. Since the reign of Pharnaces (son of Mithridates), the army of the Bosporan Kingdom started to include an increasing number of Sarmatians, who gradually substituted the Scythians as the main component of Bosporan forces. The increasing influence of the Sarmatians during the first century of Roman 'protection' over Greek Crimea transformed the Bosporan Army into a cavalry force supported by minor contingents of infantry (mostly archers). The core of the mounted troops was represented by the heavy cavalry, which was formed by cataphracts equipped in Sarmatian fashion, although mounted archers were also employed. The few infantry included some heavy units (equipped like Roman legionaries) and some light ones.

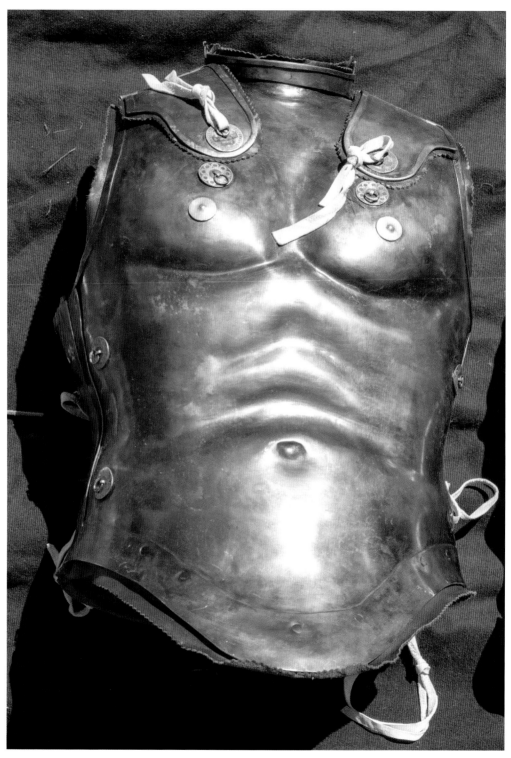

Detail of a leather muscle cuirass. (*Photo and copyright by Hetairoi*)

Chapter 12

The Epirote Army

The history of Epirus was very similar in many aspects to that of Macedonia: located at the northern borders of the Greek world, this region of the Balkans (more or less corresponding to modern Albania) was strongly influenced by both the Illyrians and Greeks. As with Macedonia, the original semi-barbarous Epirus gradually transformed into a 'hellenized' kingdom, thus becoming one of the most significant Hellenistic states. Traditionally, Epirus had always been inhabited by three main tribes: the Chaonians in the north, the Molossians in the centre and the Thesprotians in the south. Until 370 BC, these three tribes were not organized into a real state and were frequently at war with each other. Unlike Greece, Epirus had no cities: all the Epirotes lived in small villages dispersed across the countryside. The three tribes of Epirus had originally been nomadic groups, constantly at war against the Illyrians from the north. This political situation continued to exist until 370 BC, when the Molossians (the most important of the three Epirote tribes) started to expand at the expense of the other two tribal groups. After some years of internal wars, the Molossians were finally able to unify Epirus and form a centralized kingdom that was ruled by the Molossian royal family of the Aecides. After some decades, the new Kingdom of Epirus decided to form an alliance with the Kingdom of Macedonia. The latter was becoming increasingly powerful militarily and the Epirotes needed an ally against the Illyrians. As a result, Neoptolemus I, the first monarch of unified Epirus, married his daughter, Olympia, to Philip of Macedon in 357 BC. When Neoptolemus died, the throne was inherited by his brother, Arybbas, who was later driven into exile by Philip of Macedon and replaced by Neoptolemus' son, Alexander. The latter was brother of Olympia and thus uncle of Alexander the Great. While his more famous nephew was conquering the Persian Empire, Alexander of Epirus decided to obtain some glory for himself by launching a military campaign in Italy. Epirus was very near to southern Italy and thus became increasingly involved in the local conflicts of the peninsula. In 334 BC, Alexander of Epirus landed in Italy, officially to help the important Greek colony of Taras in its war against the Italic tribes of the Lucanians and Bruttii. The campaign organized to emulate Alexander the Great, however, was a failure and Alexander of Epirus was killed in battle in 331. In the following decades, as we have seen, the Kingdom of Epirus was involved in the Wars of the Diadochi and thus temporarily abandoned any ambition of expansion in Italy.

Argive, 'pelte', round and oval shields (from left to right). (*Photo and copyright by Hetairoi*)

This situation only changed in 295 BC with the rise to the Epirote throne of Pyrrhus, who had great political ambitions. As we have seen, during the first part of his reign Pyrrhus did everything possible to conquer the Kingdom of Macedonia for himself, but the superior military capabilities of his enemies prevented him from achieving any significant success. As a result, with his original ambitions frustrated, Pyrrhus decided to follow the example of Alexander of Epirus and launched a great military expedition to 'support' Taras in southern Italy. The campaign on the peninsula, however, proved to be very difficult and costly for the Epirotes, who had to face the military power of Rome: the Kingdom of Epirus was the first Hellenistic state to fight against the Romans in battle. After achieving very little, Pyrrhus moved to Sicily to ally himself with the Greek cities of the island against the Carthaginians, who were expanding at the expense of the Greeks, with the clear intention of conquering the whole island. Pyrrhus was able to achieve remarkable success in Sicily, almost expelling the Carthaginians from the island. However, the Greek cities rebelled against him because they understood that the Epirote king only wanted to conquer Sicily for himself. Obliged to abandon Sicily, Pyrrhus marched against the Romans, but was decisively defeated at the Battle of Beneventum (275 BC), after which he decided to abandon Italy and leave Taras to face the Romans alone.

In constant search of glory, Pyrrhus resumed his political ambitions over Macedonia and Greece, soon starting a new war against Antigonus Gonatas with the objective of conquering the throne of Macedonia. He also marched into Greece, with the aim of placing some of his allies at the head of important cities like Sparta or Argos. In 272 BC, during some harsh street-fighting in Argos, Pyrrhus was killed, after which the Kingdom of Epirus quickly lost any ambition to be a military superpower and became a minor participant in the Hellenistic political struggles. In 233, the last exponent of the Aecides royal family died without heirs, leaving Epirus with no ruler. Shortly after, the Epirotes decided to transform their kingdom into a federal republic known as the Epirote League with a sort of parliament. The League remained neutral during the first two wars fought between Rome and Macedonia, but was involved in the last, decisive conflict of 171–168 BC, when the Molossians sided with Macedonia while the other two tribes sided with Rome. After the end of the war, in 167, the territories of the Molossians were annexed by Rome. The Chaonians and Thesprotians were soon transformed from allies into subjects of the Roman Republic, resulting in the disappearance of Epirus as an independent state.

Until the ascendancy of Alexander of Epirus, Epirote military forces were simply made of irregular tribal levies, which were very similar to those of the Illyrians. These contingents of light infantrymen, presumably equipped as *psiloi* skirmishers or traditional peltasts, were transformed into regular troops shortly before the first Epirote expedition to Italy. Alexander of Epirus was a personal friend and loyal ally of Philip of Macedon. He had spent most of his early life as a hostage at the Macedonian royal court, so it is highly probable that he learned how to reorganize an army from Philip of Macedon and then decided to apply the latter's military reforms in his country. Epirus was mountainous and inhospitable, with a terrain that was perfect for loose formations of light infantry and not for tightly packed heavy phalangists. In addition, unlike Macedonia or Thessaly, Epirus could field a small cavalry force formed by the few nobles of the country. Under Pyrrhus, however, the Epirote Army soon transformed into a significant military force thanks to the major use of contingents provided by allies or mercenaries. When the ambitious king landed in Italy, his expeditionary army comprised the following: 23,000 infantrymen, 2,000 archers, 500 slingers, 3,000 cavalrymen and twenty war elephants. It is interesting to note that Pyrrhus was strongly supported by Ptolemy Keraunos during the organization of his Italian expedition: the usurper of Lysimachus' dominions and army sent him the twenty war elephants and 5,500 excellent veteran soldiers. Of these, 5,000 were Macedonian phalangists who formed the real core of Pyrrhus' infantry. The heavy infantry of the Epirote Army was completed by 2,000 phalangists from the city of Ambracia (the only significant urban centre of Epirus, conquered by Pyrrhus, who made it the new capital of his kingdom) and 12,000 'real' Epirotes (Molossians, Chaonians and Thesprotians) also equipped as phalangists. The 12,000 Epirotes were organized into three different units of 4,000 men, corresponding to the three main tribal groups of Epirus. The remaining 4,000 infantry were all lightly equipped Greek mercenaries: Aitolians, Athamanians and Acarnanians. The 3,000 cavalry comprised 2,000 heavy cavalrymen from Epirus and 1,000 light cavalrymen. The 2,000 heavy cavalry was formed by the aristocracy of the kingdom, as in Macedonia, apparently comprising an elite *agema* squadron of 400 men (acting as the mounted bodyguard of the king) and eight 'line' squadrons with 200 soldiers each. The 1,000 light cavalry included 500 Thessalians sent by Ptolemy

Example of 'pelte' shield. (*Photo and copyright by Hetairoi*)

Keraunos and 500 Greek mercenaries (Aitolians, Athamanians and Acarnanians). After its arrival in Italy, the army was supplemented by the military forces of Taras and large numbers of allied/mercenary Italic warriors from several different peoples. Later, during his Sicilian campaign, Pyrrhus could count on massive numbers of local allies and mercenaries provided by the Greek cities of the island: Syracuse sent him 10,000 infantry and 400 cavalry. Most of the Italic and Sicilian mercenaries recruited during the campaigns in southern Italy were paid by Pyrrhus only thanks to the economic resources of Taras. After returning to Epirus for his last military enterprise, the ambitious king had to rebuild his army, recruiting 5,000 Galatians who had already served under Antigonus Gonatas as mercenaries (these Celts had remained in Greece after their failed invasion).

Chapter 13

The Greek Cities

A thens: The citizens of Greece's most important city were organized into ten tribes, each of which provided one regiment (*taxis*) of hoplites and one squadron (*phyle*) of cavalry. Infantry regiments numbered 1,000 soldiers each, while each cavalry squadron had 100 horsemen. During the Hellenistic period two further tribes were added to the population of Athens, bringing the total of the Athenian Army to 12,000 hoplites and 1,200 cavalrymen. Light infantry was very poor in quality and numbers, thus playing very little part in the military organization of Athens. As time progressed, thanks to the great economic capabilities of the city, Athenians started to prefer avoiding military service and began recruiting large numbers of mercenaries. After defeat in the Lamian War, the Athenian Army was strongly reduced in its numbers and started to be composed almost entirely of mercenaries. The latter were supplemented by a few volunteer citizens who decided to serve as full-time soldiers; these were known as *epilektoi* and formed a sort of military elite.

Boiotia: The Greek cities of Boiotia (or Boeotia) were organized into a military and political alliance that was led by Thebes, the most important and powerful city of the region. Until 387 BC, this confederation of Boiotian cities was structured on eleven different districts, four of which were directly controlled by Thebes. In case of war, each district was to provide 1,000 hoplites and 100 cavalrymen (bringing the total military force of the Boiotian League to 11,000 hoplites and 1,100 cavalry). Before the ascendancy of the Macedonians, Theban hoplites were considered the best soldiers in Greece, particularly the 300 elite soldiers who made up the famous Sacred Band, a regular corps of professional hoplites who acted as the garrison of Thebes' citadel. At the Battle of Chaironeia, Philip of Macedon destroyed the Sacred Band, and some years later Alexander the Great demolished the city of Thebes. After these dramatic events, the military reputation of the Boiotian League entered a long period of decay. After the Galatian invasion of Greece, the Boiotians were among the first Greeks to re-equip their hoplites as *thureophoroi*. Some decades later, in 245 BC, the Boiotian soldiers were again re-equipped as phalangists in Macedonian fashion, being the first Greeks to do this. The new phalangists of each Boiotian city were commonly known as *peltophoroi* and were supplemented by two elite infantry units, the *epilektoi* and the *agema*. The first was an elite corps formed by professional full-time soldiers, the

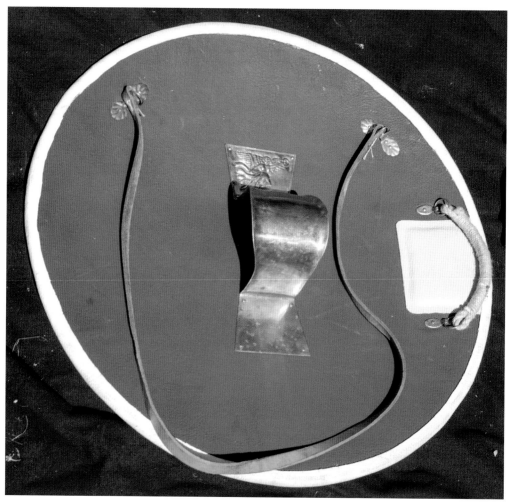

Back of a 'pelte' shield. (*Photo and copyright by Hetairoi*)

second a unit formed with the best men from the part-time citizen soldiers, who were called out when the full levy was not needed.

Sparta: After being defeated by Thebes, the Spartans had lost their military supremacy over Greece. The true Spartan citizens were only a minority caste, known as *Spartiatai*; in war these were supplemented by those living nearby in the countryside of Lakonia and by citizens from Lakonia's other cities. The former were known as helots and served as light infantrymen (being considered as serfs by the true Spartans), while the latter (*perioikoi*) served as 'second-line' hoplites. As a response to the numerical decline of the *Spartiatai*, the authorities of Sparta started to grant 'minor citizenship' to an increasing number of helots, who, in exchange for their new political rights, had to serve in the Spartan Army as hoplites (being known as *neodamodeis*). The Spartan infantry was organized into twelve battalions, or *lochoi*, each numbering 144 soldiers. The single *lochoi* were divided into two companies of seventy-two men each, known as *pentekostyes*, which were in turn composed of two *enomotiai* of thirty-six soldiers each. With six officers for each *lochos*, Sparta's infantry numbered 1,800 men (very few compared with the Spartan armies of its golden age), of whom only 1,000 were *Spartiatai*, the rest being *neodamodeis*. Similarly to Thebes' Sacred Band, Sparta had a Royal Guard formed by 300 elite hoplites (all *Spartiatai*). Cavalry were quite few and of low quality, generally including no more than 500 horsemen; mercenaries were rarely employed, the only notable exception being Cretan archers. Unlike other Greek cities such as Thebes, Sparta never re-equipped its infantry as *thureophoroi*, and until 227 BC the Spartans continued to fight as traditional hoplites. In that year king Cleomenes III re-equipped the whole Spartan heavy infantrymen as Macedonian phalangists, also giving citizenship to 4,000 *perioikoi* and including them in the new Spartan phalanx. Later, another 2,000 freed helots were included in the new phalanx of Cleomenes III. During the Hellenistic period, the number of light infantrymen provided by the helots strongly diminished, but the *perioikoi* continued to send several thousand 'traditional' hoplites. For the war against Rome in 195 BC, the Spartans were able to deploy the following troops: 10,000 phalangists (including all the *perioikoi*, who had by now received Macedonian equipment), 4,000 mercenaries and 2,000 Cretan archers. After being defeated by Rome, Sparta was forced to become a member of the Achaian League.

The Achaian League: Founded in 280 BC, this confederation of Greek cities gradually expanded over the decades and came to include all the states of the Peloponnese region. Initially the Achaian (or Achaean) League was formed to counter the remaining ambitions of Sparta, but it later became one of Rome's main opponents in Greece. Until 217 BC, the military organization of the Achaian League was very patchy. In that year, however, all the members of the confederation agreed to create a more stable military structure. This was to be based on a standing army of 11,000 infantry and 800 cavalry, the foot troops made up by 8,000 mercenaries and 3,000 citizens, while the horse troops comprised 500 mercenaries and 300 citizens. Achaia was one of the Greek regions 'exporting' the largest numbers of mercenaries in the Hellenistic world. Apparently, all citizen infantry were *thureophoroi*, who were re-equipped as phalangists in Macedonian fashion from 208 BC. During the same period the citizen cavalry was also reformed, being organized into squadrons of 100 men each. Mercenaries came from several sources, including heavy infantry *thorakitai*, Illyrian light infantrymen, Cretan archers, 'Tarantine' light cavalry and Thracian mounted skirmishers.

The Aetolian League: Since the early periods of Greek history, the region of Aetolia had been quite poor. Unlike other areas of Greece, Aetolia had no large cities and most

Example of Argive shield. (*Photo and copyright by Hetairoi*)

of the local inhabitants lived in small villages dispersed over the countryside. They were grouped into a confederation known as the Aetolian League around 370 BC. As a result of these peculiarities, Aetolian infantrymen were all lightly equipped as traditional peltasts and not as hoplites. Apparently, the warlike peoples of central Greece were accustomed to fight in mountainous terrain and thus provided excellent contingents of light infantry. Aetolians were famous as pirates and brigands, being considered the most 'barbarous' of all the Greeks. Aetolia was unique in Greece in another aspect: differently from most other political entities, the Aetolian League made practically no use of mercenaries. In fact Aetolia 'exported' some of the largest numbers of mercenaries in the Hellenistic world. In case of full mobilization, the Aetolian League could deploy a total of 12,000 infantry and 1,000 cavalry. Among the infantrymen,

300 were organized into an elite unit of *epilektoi*. Over time, an increasing number of Aetolian infantrymen started to be re-equipped as hoplites, but this process was never fully completed because after the Galatian invasion all Aetolian foot troops were re-equipped as *thureophoroi*. During Rome's campaigns in Greece, the Aetolian League was a loyal ally of the Romans against the rival Achaian League.

Taras: The Greek colonies of southern Italy were very numerous and generally quite rich, having flourished thanks to commerce with the local Italic tribes that inhabited the central mountainous areas of the region. For many of the Greek colonies, however, the Italic tribes were a serious menace. The Greeks had only colonized the coastal areas of the region and had never been able to submit the local warrior peoples (Samnites, Apulians, Lucanians and Bruttii). Over time, another menace started to appear on the horizon: the expansionism of the Roman Republic. Taras (or Tarentum), the most important and rich city among the Greek colonies of southern Italy, had to face both the Italic peoples and the Romans during the space of a few decades. As we have seen, on both occasions Taras asked for help and received major military support from the nearby Kingdom of Epirus. Both the Epirote expeditions, however, were failures from a military point of view, and the second led to the Roman conquest of Taras in 272 BC. Regarding the military organization of Taras, we should bear in mind that the city was Sparta's only overseas colony, having been founded in 706 BC. This had some important consequences on the military structures adopted by the Tarantines. Unlike many of the Greek colonies in Italy, Taras had a solid democratic constitution that provided a high degree of internal stability.

From a military point of view, the Tarantines were more or less the Italian equivalent of the Thessalians in Greece: controlling part of Apulia's large plains, Taras could deploy large numbers of excellent cavalrymen (mostly having light equipment). As we have already seen, the Tarantine horsemen started to be employed as mercenaries in every corner of the Hellenistic world and soon acquired a great reputation. Over the decades the term 'Tarantine' started to indicate all Greek mercenaries being equipped like the original light cavalrymen from Taras. The word 'Tarantine' no longer bore a geographical significance but was used purely as a tactical term to indicate a precise category of troops. 'Tarantine' horsemen were light skirmishers equipped similarly to the Thessalians, but in addition to the traditional javelins they also wore a helmet and carried a shield (round or oval). They were a new category of 'medium' cavalry, with no armour but with some capabilities to conduct close combat (thanks to the helmet and shield). They were a mounted equivalent of the foot *thureophoroi*, since they could act both as simple skirmishers and as 'shock' cavalry (albeit with minor impact compared with the Macedonian heavy cavalry). The army of Taras comprised a phalanx of 20,000 men, 3,000 light cavalry and 1,000 heavy cavalry. The Tarantine phalangists were all

Back of an Argive shield. (*Photo and copyright by Hetairoi*)

equipped with white metal shields and were thus commonly known as *Leukaspides*. It is highly probable that it was Alexander of Epirus who re-equipped the Tarantine hoplites as phalangists and gave them these white shields during his unsuccessful Italian campaign. The 1,000 heavy cavalry (*hipparchoi*) formed a separate unit from the light horsemen, who were considered the real elite of the Tarantine Army. Thanks to the great economic resources deriving from trade, the Tarantines could supplement their forces with large numbers of mercenaries, which were either Greek (mostly Spartans) or Italic (from the same tribes that fought against Taras).

Syracuse: The Greek colonies in Sicily were even richer than those located in mainland southern Italy, but had to face an enemy that was much more powerful than the Italic tribes of the peninsula. The Phoenicians had started to found their own colonies in the western part of the island from 734 BC. When these came under the political leadership of Carthage, Syracuse and the other Greek cities started to fight several wars against the newcomers in order to limit their expansionist ambitions. It soon became clear that Carthage in North Africa wanted to conquer the whole of Sicily in order to control the most important commercial routes of the Mediterranean Sea. Syracuse, being the most important and richest of all the Greek colonies on the island, was the main target of the Carthaginians. The city had been founded by the Corinthians in 733 BC, soon becoming very large. Due to the constant menace represented by the foreign invaders, the city of Syracuse was mostly ruled by tyrants and had only very short experiences of democratic government. Only tyrants could have strong enough authority to resist the Carthaginians effectively. The two most successful tyrants of Syracuse were Agathokles (who ruled from 317-289 BC) and Hieron (270-215 BC), both of whom tried to expand the power of their city over the other Greek colonies of Sicily and at the same time opposed the Carthaginians. During the First Punic War, Syracuse acted as a loyal ally of Rome, but the city allied with Carthage in the Second Punic War and was finally conquered by the Romans (along with the rest of Sicily) in 212 BC.

The Syracusan Army was mostly formed by mercenaries during the whole Hellenistic period; the former citizen soldiers who had defeated the Athenians during the Peloponnesian War were only a distant memory. Due to the increasing wealth derived from commerce, the tyrants of Syracuse preferred recruiting impressive bodies of mercenaries instead of obliging their citizens to serve (which could have caused the outbreak of internal revolts). This started to happen on a regular basis during the reign of Dionysius I (405-367 BC). Syracuse, thanks to superior economic capabilities, was the only Greek colony of Sicily that could recruit and maintain an entire army of mercenaries. Like the Carthaginians, the Syracusans recruited the best mercenaries of the western Mediterranean from a wide variety of sources. The mercenaries serving Syracuse usually served in distinct units formed according to their nationality, being commanded by their own officers and equipped in their native style. At the time of Agathokles, the Syracusan Army on campaign could field the following troops: 3,500 Syracusan hoplites, 2,500 allied hoplites (sent by other Greek cities of Sicily), 1,000 chosen mercenary hoplites (Greeks who formed Agathokles' personal guard), 1,000 Samnite mercenaries, 1,000 Etruscan mercenaries, 1,000 Gallic

Example of light infantry round shield. (*Photo and copyright by Hetairoi*)

mercenaries, 500 missile troops (archers or slingers) and 800 cavalrymen. With these impressive forces, Agathokles even managed to launch a military campaign in North Africa, with the objective of conquering Carthage. In many respects, the Syracusan Army was a private military force (*hetairia*) serving the tyrant who was currently in power. Its core was represented by the 1,000 chosen mercenaries, a permanent corps of professional soldiers who served under every tyrant. Mercenaries also came from other sources, in addition to those listed above: there were Cretan archers, Sikels (the Italic native inhabitants of Sicily), Iberians (formerly in the service of Carthage), Ligurians and Oscans (a broad term including Samnites, Lucanians and Bruttii). The Oscans, in particular, were known for their incredible valour and great cruelty. Several of them, at the end of their period of service, decided to remain in Sicily and thus formed their own settlements/military colonies.

Agathokles recruited several thousand Oscans, who became a problem after his death in 289 BC, remaining in Sicily without any occupation and deciding to conquer the city of Messana for themselves. Messana controlled the straits dividing Sicily from peninsular Italy, and was thus probably the most strategically important location of the island. The Oscans, after taking the city, started to call themselves 'Mamertini' ('Sons of Mars') and initiated heavy tolls on all the ships passing through the straits. The Mamertini dominated Messana for over twenty years, during which they transformed themselves into real pirates. For a period they even allied themselves with the city of Rhegion, which was located across from Messana on the other side of the straits. Rhegion had also been occupied by a group of Oscan renegades, an allied legion of Italic soldiers who had mutinied after having been sent to garrison Rhegion by the Romans. In 265 BC, the Syracusan Army besieged Messana to eliminate forever the Oscan mercenaries, who sought the help of Carthage and Rome. This led to the retreat of the Syracusans and the outbreak of the First Punic War, as both Carthage and Rome wanted to occupy Messana. During the conflict, Messana was occupied by Rome and the Mamertini soon disappeared from history.

Example of *thureos* oval shield. (*Photo and copyright by Hetairoi*)

Chapter 14

Hellenistic Israel

After the death of Alexander the Great and the end of the wars between the Successors, Judaea became part of the Seleucid Empire. The Jews initially accepted Seleucid dominance with no particular problems, since their new rulers permitted them to practise their religion in peace. This situation, however, changed dramatically in 168 BC when Antiochus IV launched a major programme of forced 'hellenization' that was unacceptable for the Jews. When the Seleucid monarch ordered the abandoning of the ancestral law of the Jewish People and forbade circumcision, Judaea rose up in revolt under the charismatic leadership of Judah the Maccabee. The ensuing conflict between the Maccabees and the Seleucids was extremely violent, with victories and defeats on both sides. Initially, Judah the Maccabee was able to defeat the Seleucids in a series of small engagements, thanks to an intelligent use of guerrilla warfare. After these victories, he was even able to enter Jerusalem in 164 BC. In 161 BC, however, the Jewish rebels were defeated by the Seleucids in a large battle. For a time the new freedom of Judaea seemed to be menaced, but the Jews were able to resist and maintained their independence. Guided by the brother of Judah the Maccabee, Jonathan the Hasmonaean, they were able to initiate a new dynasty of kings. Taking advantage of the civil wars that ravaged the Seleucid Empire during those years, the first Hasmonaean monarch was finally able to obtain effective independence for Judaea. Formally, however, the Jews remained subjects of the Seleucids until the reign of John Hyrcanus I (135-107 BC), one of the greatest Hasmonaean kings, who obtained formal independence from the Seleucids and even expanded his kingdom by conquering new territories, such as Idumaea in the south, which was inhabited by warlike Arab nomads. In just a few decades, Judaea became an important regional power with great political ambitions.

In 66 BC, however, civil war broke out after the death of King Alexander Janneus and his wife, Salome Alexandra. The throne of Judaea was contended between the two sons of the former king, named Hyrcanus II and Aristobulos II. Hyrcanus was supported by one of his father's most important courtiers, Antipater the Idumaean. In 63 BC, both brothers asked for the military intervention of the Romans, who had a large army in nearby Syria under the command of Pompey the Great. The latter decided to intervene in favour of Hyrcanus and quickly defeated the supporters of

Back of a *thureos* oval shield. (*Photo and copyright by Hetairoi*)

Aristobulos. The Roman help obviously had a high price: in 57 BC, Judaea was divided into five small, self-governing territories that were all client states of Rome. In 40 BC, Judaea was invaded by the Parthians, who had already defeated Roman military forces in Syria. The invaders wanted to reunite the country under their own puppet king, Antigonus II (son of Aristobulos II, the pretender defeated by Pompey). Herod the Great, son of Antipater the Idumaean, decided to fight against the superior forces of the Parthians and of their client king. Against all odds, Herod was able to defeat Antigonus II after three years of war and reconquered the whole of Judaea thanks to Roman help. Under Herod the Great the Jewish Army became an excellent military force and conducted several victorious campaigns of territorial expansion (most notably against the Nabataeans). Herod was Rome's most important ally in the Middle East and was even able to fight on equal terms against the Ptolemaic military forces of Cleopatra. When the great king died in 4 BC, however, Judaea was divided between the three sons of the former king, forming three small and self-governing territories that were all client states of Rome. The most important of these was annexed by the Romans in AD 6, being followed by the other two in AD 39 and 94.

The military forces initially raised by Judah the Maccabee had very little organization to speak of, being entirely composed of insurgents equipped as light infantry skirmishers. These numbered just 6,000 men, but later expanded to 20,000. Thanks to a deep knowledge of Hellenistic military tactics, the Maccabees were able to defeat the larger Seleucid Army on several occasions. After these victories, Judah the Maccabee started to organize his men into units of 1,000 soldiers each, which were in turn divided into hundreds, fifties and tens. Apparently, a number of the Jewish soldiers started to be trained and re-equipped as phalangists, while some sort of cavalry was also formed. According to the most recent studies, this 'professionalization' of the Jewish rebel forces was carried on under the supervision of ex-Jewish soldiers who had served the Ptolemies (see earlier chapter on the Ptolemaic Army). These veterans had returned to Judaea to help their country when the revolt against the Seleucids broke out. The Hasmonaean kings who succeeded Judah the Maccabee transformed their infantry into *thureophoroi*, who continued to be organized into units of 1,000 men. Each infantry corps was supported by a squadron of 200 light horsemen, which was divided into four 'fifties'. There were twenty-three units of *thureophoroi*, with 23,000 infantrymen and 4,600 light horsemen supporting them. The cavalry was completed by 1,400 heavy horsemen, organized into fourteen squadrons with 100 men each. Finally, there were 5,000 foot skirmishers (archers or slingers) in five units of 1,000 men. In total, the Hasmonaean Army could deploy 28,000 infantry and 6,000 cavalry. Until the ascendancy of Herod the Great, foreign allies or mercenaries were rarely employed due to nationalistic and religious issues.

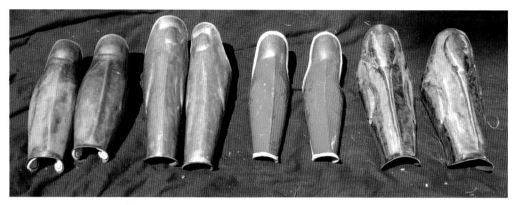

Different models of Hellenistic bronze greaves. (*Photo and copyright by Hetairoi*)

Despite being the military force of a client state of Rome, the army of Herod the Great was a proper Hellenistic military apparatus that was characterized by a very multinational nature. When Herod became king, the Jewish Army started to enjoy a privileged position in the state and soon became one of the main pillars of Herodian power. In practical terms, the oath of allegiance of the new Jewish Army created by Herod was to the king and not to the population of the country; as a result, we could define it as a 'private' military force. Most of its superior officers came from the same family of Herod or were Roman/Italic 'advisors' sent by the Roman authorities. The Herodian Army included three different kinds of unit: the heavy infantry regiment (named *meros*, each including 3,000 soldiers), the light infantry regiment (*telos*, 2,000 men) and the cavalry squadron (*ile*, 200 soldiers). From an ethnic point of view, the Herodian Army could be divided into two main components: the Jewish one (the majority, including troops of standard quality) and the Gentile one (the minority, including troops of superior quality). Gentiles were all the non-Jews living in ancient Judaea. It is important to note that the Jewish troops also included the Idumaeans, who had converted to Hebraism after their land was conquered by John Hyrcanus I. The family of Herod was Idumaean, and thus Idumaeans were always the most loyal 'native' soldiers serving Herod. In total, at its maximum expansion, the Herodian Army could deploy 25,000 men (20,000 infantry and 5,000 cavalry). These came from a variety of sources, which generally corresponded to different troop types. Generally speaking, Roman influence over the Herodian Army was quite strong, especially regarding heavy infantry and engineers, both of which were organized and trained under the supervision of Roman military advisors. The Herodian Army included a large Royal Guard, which comprised more or less 2,000 men: Idumaeans, Thracians, Galatians and Germans. The last three groups were mercenaries. The Idumaean bodyguards were known as *doryphoroi* and were either aristocratic young men or distinguished veteran soldiers from Herod's home region. Thracians had already been employed as mercenaries by the Hasmonaean kings of the previous decades, while Galatians had a more interesting history; apparently they had been part of Cleopatra's Ptolemaic Army until 30 BC, and were then assigned to Herod by Augustus as a reward for his loyalty. Regarding the Germans, Herod probably recruited them following the example of Augustus, who had a small personal bodyguard of 500 warriors from Germany (the *germani corporis custodes*). Each of the four ethnic groups forming the Royal Guard was organized into an independent unit of 500 soldiers, and apparently all the bodyguards of Herod were able to serve both as infantry and cavalry.

The heavy infantrymen of the Herodian Army were equipped as *thorakitai/* imitation legionaries and were called *sebastenoi*. It seems these were organized into a single regiment of 3,000 soldiers, which was supported by 500 heavy horsemen (equipped like the legionary cavalrymen of the Roman Army). As is clear from this brief description, the *sebastenoi* were more or less the equivalent of a Roman legion. The rest of the infantrymen were all equipped as *thureophoroi* or as light skirmishers (javelineers and archers). The best of the light infantry contingents were provided by the Idumaeans and the Ituraeans, both of whom were nomadic and of Arab descent, having been forcibly converted to Hebraism after their countries were invaded by the Hasmonaean kings. Apparently, however, a good number of the Ituraeans came from outside the borders of Herod's kingdom, in particular from the area of present-day Lebanon. As a result, these were still Gentiles and served in the Jewish Army as mercenaries. Idumaean and Ituraean archers were considered to be among the best of the Middle East, also being appreciated by the Romans.

The cavalry was mostly formed by light cavalrymen, plus an elite corps of 600 horse archers who were equipped in Parthian fashion with composite bow. These mounted archers were known as Babylonian cavalrymen in the Herodian Army, apparently because the unit was formed with Jews from Babylon. We don't know why, but these 600 Babylonian Jews at some point decided to abandon their home city and moved to Judaea. Since they had already served in the Parthian Army as mounted archers, they transferred their military expertise to the service of Herod. The latter settled them in his kingdom as military colonists, giving grants of land in exchange for military service. The Babylonian cavalrymen were not the only soldiers settled in his kingdom as military colonists by Herod the Great: several military settlements of loyal Idumaeans were created in the border regions of Herod's territories. Adopting the system that had been employed for centuries by the other Hellenistic monarchs, Herod wanted to prevent the outbreak of revolts in the most turbulent areas of his kingdom. The military colonists acted both as a national reserve that could be mobilized in case of necessity and as garrison forces protecting the borders of Judaea. When Herod died

Hellenistic bronze greaves. (*Photo and copyright by Hetairoi*)

Different models of Hellenistic boots and sandals. (*Photo and copyright by Hetairoi*)

in 4 BC, the population of his kingdom rose up in revolt, most of the soldiers siding with the rebels against the Romans, with the exception of the Royal Guard and heavy infantry *sebastenoi*. After the suppression of the rebellion, the Herodian Army was finally disbanded by the Romans, while the members of the Royal Guard and *sebastenoi* who had remained loyal to Rome were absorbed into the Roman Army and organized into new units of auxiliaries. The small Jewish states that continued to exist after the death of Herod had some small military forces, but these were of very little combat value. When the Jews revolted again against the Romans in AD 66, these small local contingents sided with Rome, and they finally disappeared from history in AD 94.

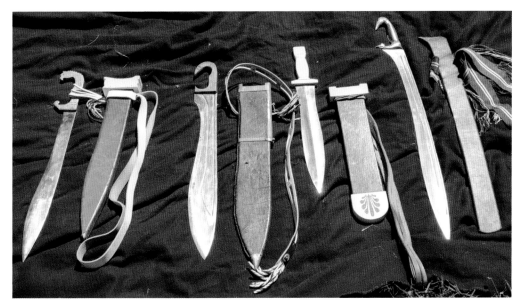

Different models of Hellenistic swords; the third from the left is a *xiphos* with straight blade, while the other three are different versions of *kopis* with forward-curving blade. (*Photo and copyright by Hetairoi*)

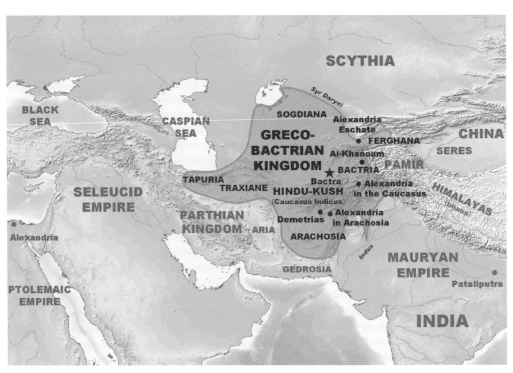

The Greco–Bactrian Kingdom. (*CC BY-SA 3.0, Wikimedia User 'World Imaging'*)

Chapter 15

The Greco-Bactrian Kingdom and the Indo-Greek Kingdom

Around 250 BC, Diodotus, the Seleucid satrap of Bactria and Sogdia (the easternmost part of the Hellenistic world, corresponding to modern central Asia and Afghanistan), decided to secede from the Seleucid Empire and founded a new independent Hellenistic state known as the Greco-Bactrian Kingdom. The new kingdom was extremely rich, since it was full of natural resources and controlled the vitally important trade routes connecting the Mediterranean with China and India. At this time Parthia, corresponding to modern Iran, also declared independence from the Seleucid Empire, eliminating any territorial link between Bactria and the Seleucids and ensuring that the new independent kingdom created by Diodotus would survive over the following decades. From the beginning of its existence, the Greco-Bactrian Kingdom was naturally an ally of the Parthians against the Seleucids. In 210 BC, the Seleucid monarch Antiochus III launched a major campaign in the east against the Parthians and Bactrians, but the alliance formed by the latter was able to resist. Parthia later formally submitted (albeit for a short time) to the Seleucids, while the Bactrian Kingdom was officially recognized by Antiochus III with the signing of a peace treaty. Soon after the death of Alexander the Great, the regions of northern India that had been occupied by the Macedonians were reconquered by Chandragupta, one of the greatest monarchs in the history of India and founder of the new Mauryan dynasty. Over time, the Mauryan Empire of India developed strong commercial and political relations with the Bactrian Kingdom, while the Mauryan monarchs also sent hundreds of their emissaries to Bactria with the objective of converting the local population to Buddhism.

This prosperous situation of peace and religious respect came to an end when the powerful Mauryan Empire collapsed and northern India divided into many smaller kingdoms. Around 180 BC, in order to obtain some benefits from the new political situation in India, the Greco-Bactrians launched an invasion of the Indian sub-continent. This was led by Demetrius I, probably the most ambitious and capable of all the Greco-Bactrian kings. By 175 BC, the Bactrians had conquered a large portion of northern India, but when Demetrius I returned to his kingdom he found a usurper named Eucratides on his throne. As a result, a civil war broke out between the usurper

Different models of Hellenistic swords; the first from the left is a *xiphos* with straight blade, while the other three are different versions of *kopis* with forward-curving blade. (*Photo and copyright by Hetairoi*)

and the legitimate royal family of the Bactrian Kingdom. At the end of the hostilities, Eucratides remained as the ruler of Bactria, initiating his own new dynasty. His opponents retained control of the newly conquered Indian territories and seceded from Bactria by establishing the independent Indo-Greek Kingdom. During this time the Bactrians were defeated on several occasions by the Parthians, who were expanding their dominions after becoming fully independent from Seleucid rule. Some years after the military campaigns against the Parthians, the Bactrian Kingdom was finally crushed and occupied by two nomadic peoples of the steppes from Central Asia: the Saka and the Yuezhi. By 120 BC, the Bactrian Kingdom was no longer in existence.

The Indo-Greek Kingdom. (*Public domain pictures from Wikimedia Commons*)

Before the arrival of the Macedonians, the local military forces of Bactria were almost entirely composed of cavalry, either lightly armed with javelins and bows or cataphracts. After the Macedonian conquest of the Persian Empire, both Alexander the Great and Seleucus settled large numbers of Macedonian/Greek military colonists in the border provinces of Bactria and Sogdia. It seems that the military settlers of these isolated regions were mostly Greeks and not Macedonians, because

Thracian sword and falx (*rhomphaia*). (*Photo and copyright by Hetairoi*)

the Hellenistic kings preferred to settle the latter into the more central areas of their dominions, such as Syria. According to the latest research, the Greek colonists in Bactria and Sogdia numbered some 20,000–25,000. The Bactrian Army was a very multinational force, formed by the Greek military settlers (who provided the heavy infantry of the phalanx) and the local Bactrian/Sogdian levies (providing light infantry, cataphracts and light cavalry). These were supplemented by considerable numbers of Greek mercenaries and Asian allies, who were mostly equipped as light infantry: the former were generally armed as traditional peltasts or as *thureophoroi*, while the latter were usually employed as skirmishers (javelineers, archers or slingers). It seems that the two most important components of the Bactrian Army were the cavalry (which was very numerous and of excellent quality) and the elephant corps (which was provided with pachyderms from nearby India). When Antiochus III tried to reconquer the Bactrian Kingdom in 208 BC, he had to face a Bactrian Army of 10,000 cavalry: the majority of these were light horsemen, but a number of heavy cataphracts were surely also deployed. These heavy cavalry were members of the local aristocracy and were considered a real elite, superior to the Greek colonists/phalangists. After the campaign in Bactria, the Seleucids decided

Detail of a *kopis* sword. (*Photo and copyright by Hetairoi*)

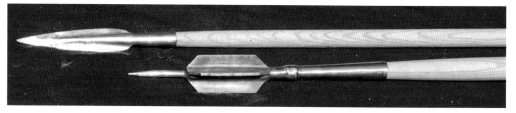

Head and butt-spike of a 'sarissa' spear. (*Photo and copyright by Hetairoi*)

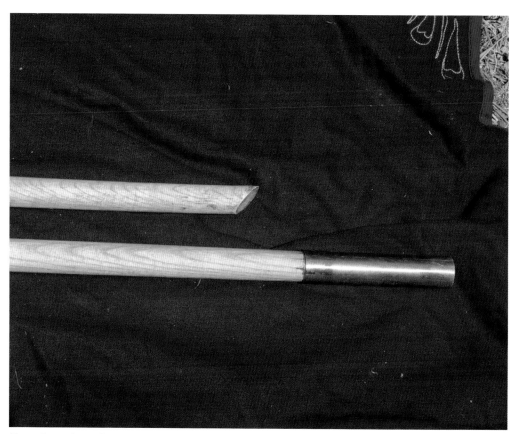

Central section of a 'sarissa' spear, where the two parts of the weapon were joined together. (*Photo and copyright by Hetairoi*)

Hellenistic light infantry javelins. (*Photo and copyright by Hetairoi*)

to transform their own heavy cavalry into proper cataphracts: the combination of Greek phalangists and Bactrian heavy cavalry had impressed Antiochus III with its efficiency. It is important to note, however, that the numerous cavalry of the Bactrian Kingdom also included an elite regiment of 'horse companions', formed of 3,000 Greek military settlers. Of these, 300 formed a chosen Royal Squadron that acted as mounted bodyguard of the king. The 7,000 native cavalrymen were presumably organized into regiments of 1,000 men each, which were locally known as *hipparchiai*. Mercenary/allied Asian cavalry were also employed, being provided by different populations, including eastern Iranians, Saka and Yuezhi. Unfortunately, we have very few details about the number of war elephants deployed by the Bactrian Greeks. What we know for sure, however, is that the peace treaty concluded by Antiochus III with the Bactrians obliged the latter to cede their entire elephant corps of fifty beasts to the Seleucids.

When the Indo-Greek Kingdom became independent from Bactria, its kings converted to Buddhism and adopted Indian culture, their realm becoming a great example of perfect fusion between the elements of two different civilizations. The greatest of the Indo-Greek monarchs was Menander I, who expanded his kingdom by conquering large territories in India. After the fall of Bactria in the north, for some time the Indo-Greeks were able to have positive relations with the Saka and Yuezhi. After 95 BC, however, the Indo-Greek Kingdom was fragmented into several small realms that were constantly at war against each other. By AD 10, all these small Indo-Greek states had been conquered by foreign invaders. Those located in the west were the first to fall, being occupied by the nomad Saka and Yuezhi, while those in the east were the last to disappear, conquered by the nearby Indian states. The Indo-Greek Army is the lesser known of all the Hellenistic military forces, but we do know that it was mostly formed by Indians. Unlike Bactria, northern India had never been colonized by Greek/Macedonian military settlers. The few Greeks of the region represented only the small ruling class of the Indo-Greek Kingdom. In addition, the secession from Bactria prevented the local Indo-Greek rulers from importing Macedonian/Greek colonists or mercenaries from the Hellenistic world. Obviously, as for all the other Indian armies of the time, the most important component of the Indo-Greek Army was the elephants, while the infantry was very numerous but lightly armed, including large numbers of archers. In total, at its maximum territorial extent, the Indo-Greek Kingdom could deploy 60,000 infantrymen, 1,000 cavalrymen and 700 war elephants. The 1,000 cavalry were probably the only Greeks of the whole army, forming an elite regiment of heavy cavalry that also acted as bodyguard of the king. As time progressed, large numbers of Saka and Yuezhi mercenary cavalrymen started to be employed as a result of the latters' migrations into India.

Hellenistic military standard reproducing Hercules. (*Photo and copyright by Hetairoi*)

Bibliography

Primary sources
Appian, *Roman History*
Arrian, *Anabasis of Alexander*
Arrian, *Indike*
Arrian, *Tactics*
Asklepiodotos, *Tactics*
Diodorus Siculus, *History*
Dionysios of Halikarnassos, *Roman Antiquities*
Livy, *History of Rome from its foundation*
Pausanias, *Guide to Greece*
Plutarch, *Lives*
Polyainos, *Stratagems*
Polybius, *The Histories*
Quintus Curtius, *History of Alexander*
Silius Italicus, *Punica*
Strabo, *Geography*
Xenophon, *Anabasis*
Xenophon, *Hellenica*
Xenophon, *Kyropaidia*
Xenophon, *On horsemanship*
Xenophon, *The cavalry commander*

Secondary sources – books
Baker, P., *Armies and Enemies of Imperial Rome* (Wargames Research Group, 1981)
Bar-Kochva, B., *The Seleucid Army* (Cambridge University Press, 1976)
Brzezinski, R. and Mielczarek, M., *The Sarmatians 600 BC–AD 450* (Osprey Publishing, 2002)
Cernenko, E.V., *The Scythians 700–300 BC* (Osprey Publishing, 1983)
Connolly, P., *Greece and Rome at War* (Frontline Books, 1981)
Fields, N., *Tarentine Horsemen of Magna Graecia* (Osprey Publishing, 2008)
Gorelik, K., *Warriors of Eurasia* (Montvert Publishing, 1995)
Head, D., *Armies of the Macedonian and Punic Wars* (Wargames Research Group, 1982)
Heckel, W. and Jones, R., *Macedonian Warrior* (Osprey Publishing, 2006)
Mielczarek, M., *The Army of the Bosporan Kingdom* (Akanthina, 1999)
Nikorov, V.P., *The Armies of Bactria 700 BC–450 AD* (Montvert Publishing, 1997)
Rocca, S., *The Army of Herod the Great* (Osprey Publishing, 2009)
Sekunda, N., *The Army of Alexander the Great* (Osprey Publishing, 1984)
Sekunda, N., *The Seleucid Army* (Montvert Publishing, 1994)
Sekunda, N., *The Ptolemaic Army* (Montvert Publishing, 1995)

Sekunda, N., *Macedonian Armies after Alexander 323–168 BC* (Osprey Publishing, 2012)
Thion, S., *Le Soldat Lagide* (LRT Editions, 2013)
Webber, C., *The Thracians 700 BC-AD 46* (Osprey Publishing, 2001)

Secondary sources – articles
Anderson, E., 'Origins of armored cavalry: the Seleucid cataphract', *Ancient Warfare Magazine*, volume V, issue 6
Beazley, M., 'Thorakitai: armed after the Roman fashion', *Ancient Warfare Magazine*, volume X, issue 2
Beek, A.L., 'Pontic sea-dogs: the pirates of Mithridates', *Ancient Warfare Magazine*, volume X, issue 3
Dean, S.E., 'Cataphracts: heavy cavalry of the Mithridatic Wars', *Ancient Warfare Magazine*, volume X, issue 3
DeSantis, M.G., 'Old men's war: the Silver Shields after Alexander', *Ancient Warfare Magazine*, volume IX, issue 5
Esposito, G., 'The Army of Antiochus IV: organization and structure of the late Seleucid Army', *Ancient Warfare Magazine*, volume VIII, issue 4
Evers, R., 'A one-man army: the forces of Epirus', *Ancient Warfare Magazine*, volume VI, issue 4
Hillen, A., 'Citizen soldiers in the Hellenistic Age: the rise and fall of the Achaean League', Ancient Warfare Magazine, volume IX, issue 5
Kambouris, M.E., 'The Hypaspist Corps', *Ancient Warfare Magazine*, volume IX, issue 5
Lobacz, M., 'At the edge of Hellenism: Armies of the Greeks in Bactria and India', *Ancient Warfare Magazine*, volume IV, issue 6
McDonnel-Staff, P., 'Hypaspists to Peltasts: the elite guard infantry of the Antigonid Macedonian Army', *Ancient Warfare Magazine*, volume V, issue 6
Olshanetsky, H., 'Warriors of Zion: Jewish soldiers in Hellenistic armies', *Ancient Warfare Magazine*, volume IX, issue 5
Post, R., 'Bright colours and uniformity: Hellenistic military costume', *Ancient Warfare Magazine*, volume IV, issue 6
Rostaing, N., 'Lost Pontic legions: Pontic imitation legions used by Mithridates', *Ancient Warfare Magazine*, volume X, issue 3
Taylor, M.J., 'The Macedonian conscription diagramma', *Ancient Warfare Magazine*, volume IX, issue 5
Vasseghi, S., 'Specialists of a polyglot army: Mithridates' elite units', *Ancient Warfare Magazine*, volume V, issue 6
Webber, C., 'Fighting on all sides: Thracian mercenaries of the Hellenistic Era', *Ancient Warfare Magazine*, volume IV, issue 6

The Re-enactors who Contributed to this Book

Hetairoi e.V.

Hetairoi e.V. is an association of people who have taken interest in various aspects of ancient Greek life and culture. Our goal is to recreate as many aspects as possible of the lives of people in ancient Greece, as well as in neighbouring cultures. Our chosen method is called 'Living History', a concept developed out of battle re-enactments. Unlike re-enactments, Living History interpreters make use of the so-called 'third-person interpretation', where they wear recreated clothing and equipment, but remain available for the audience to answer any questions and explain their activities. Sometimes short historical scenes are re-enacted, usually narrated by a member of the group explaining what is happening to the audience.

As of 2019, our members are able to show reconstructions from the early Classical era, around 500 BC, to the late Hellenistic period, around 100 BC. Because you can't fully understand a culture without studying its neighbours, we have also recreated historical impressions from the important Greek neighbours of Rome, Persia, southern Italy, Thrace and Scythia. It is very important that the reconstructed equipment and clothing are based on the historic originals as closely as possible. We strive to base our recreations on the latest state of scientific research and invest a lot of time in research before starting our work. If we can't craft the pieces ourselves, our reconstructed equipment is sometimes created by craftsmen, who are specialized in reconstructions for museums.

The Hetairoi are at your service for events in museums or educational institutions, or other events where the transfer of knowledge is the main focus. As such we have among others already collaborated with museums such as the Ephesos Museum and the Kunsthistorisches Museum in Vienna, the Reiss-Engelhorn-Museen in Mannheim, the Varusschlacht Museum und Park Kalkriese and the Historisches Museum der Pfalz in Speyer.

Contacts:
E-mail: info@hetairoi.de
Website: http://hetairoi.de
Facebook: https://www.facebook.com/Hetairoi.de

Index